To Kyanne,

Make the most
of your Life!

Isaac Fernandez

4-26-89

I don't want much from life... WANT MORE

by Joan Kennedy

FREDERICK FELL PUBLISHERS, INC.
NEW YORK

Fell Edition 1980

For information address:

Frederick Fell Publishers, Inc.
386 Park Avenue South
New York, New York 10016

Book designed by Ralph Daddio

MANUFACTURED IN THE UNITED STATES OF AMERICA

ISBN 0-8119-0335-4

With love
  to my children
    Bob
    Marnie
    Patty
    Amy

CONTENTS

3

ACKNOWLEDGEMENTS

I owe a special debt of gratitude to Ralph Daddio, for his suggestions and high competence in assisting at all stages of this book.

A special thanks to Nancy Dodge Dow, for her invaluable assistance in editing this book.

Finally, my thanks to Michael Stevenson, for his delightful illustrations.

PREFACE

In this ever-changing world, many of us complain that we are not able to do anything about our circumstances; yet the fact remains that many of us do the things we choose to do. Even though we may want to go a certain way, we allow ourselves to follow the old way because it offers the least resistance.

Sometimes, it is a crisis that forces us out of our comfortable old ways into a re-evaluation.

JOAN KENNEDY

Part One

"*If we had no winter,
The spring would
not be so pleasant:
If we did not
sometimes taste
of adversity,
prosperity
would not be
so welcome.*"

ANNE BRADSTREET

11

Life Beyond The Kitchen

CHAPTER ONE

ONE bitter cold morning as I drove to a part-time job in a car which had a heater that no longer functioned, I finally reached a point in my life when I felt I had lost all hope for the future.

At forty-five my life was cut and dried. Nothing was ever going to happen to change the endless days and nights that stretched out before me.

For twenty years my married life had fluctuated between feelings of frustration and contentment. When I was frustrated, I took down walls, moved furniture, changed my kitchen curtains, and went antiquing. When I was content, I vacuumed, dusted, and baked cookies.

I remember a gathering of friends at my home

for one of our weekly coffee klatches. During the course of our conversation, I remarked that I was content, and one of my friends turned to me and said, "Joan, only cows are contented."

As I review the years when I was raising my children, I was forever busy; decorating, moving furniture, braiding rugs, quilting, painting and papering. As my children grew and my spare time increased, so did my activities - antiquing, refinishing furniture, volunteer work, and moving *more* furniture.

The decorating, remodeling and all the other busy work I was involved in, was an escape. I was avoiding the real conflicts within myself and in my life.

My marriage was crumbling; I had no future as far as anything tangible was concerned. I was past forty, with three children still at home, very little working background, very little education, and no money of my own.

Although my life held many uncertainties, the thought of undertaking anything as monumental as getting a job was a frightening consideration.

At the time, I didn't want to make any drastic changes. A feeling of panic would set in each time I considered giving up my familiar ways and accepting the challenge of the unknown. The thought that always surfaced was, "What will I do about tomorrow?"

During the time I was married and raising my children, I had never concerned myself with the prospects of someday looking for a job or preparing myself for one, mentally or emotionally. Like most women, I had closed all my doors after I married. I felt that there was no need for any more planning. I had arrived at the final major goal in my life - the role of wife, mother and homemaker.

I felt, as Rudyard Kipling said, that,

"There's no sense in going further - it's the edge of cultivation, so they said, and I believed it - broke my land and sowed my crop. Built my barns and strung my fences in the little border station tucked away below the foothills where the trails run out and stop.

Till a voice, as bad as conscience, rang interminal changes on one everlasting whisper day and night - go; something hidden. Go and find it. Go and look behind the ranges - something lost behind the ranges. Lost and waiting for you. Go."

If I had known what was taking place in my life, I would have realized the urgency for finding my talent and developing it. While, in reality, I was home being a mother and homemaker, in my mind I was headed for a life alone with my children. If I had realized and accepted this, I would have stopped all the busy

15

work I kept myself involved in.

Why did I feel I had to braid all my own rugs, make my own quilts, and paint my own walls? Today I do none of these. My rugs are worn out and my quilts were disintegrated by the sun's rays. The only thing that remains with me is the result of the thoughts I entertained as I braided, quilted, and painted. Those thoughts have become my present.

After many financial setbacks, I finally reached the decision to find a job. With my sketchy working experiences, however, the thoughts that kept surfacing were, "What can I possibly do?", and "Who'd want me?"

Many times I asked myself, "How could I have spent so many years on this earth and not ended up with *something* I could do to make a living for myself." For days I sat and thought about all the things I couldn't do. Now I realize that I concerned myself with the things I couldn't do because I couldn't think of anything I could do, or wanted to do.

My resume, at that period in my life, would have convinced any personnel manager that I was definitely "factory level." In an eight-year period, I worked in a tape factory, a gunsight factory, as a receptionist, and finally, as a model.

The thought of going back to factory work depressed me. I discounted the possibility of getting a job as a model. In 1966, fashion was geared to the young. I was wearing my skirts two inches below my knees and the stores were selling them four inches above the knees and higher. On me, this had the effect of "Alice in Wonderland" from the back, and "Lost Horizon" from the front. It was a foregone conclusion that the world of fashion was the last place I would try to enter.

At the suggestion of a friend, I applied for a job at the University of Minnesota. Along with my application, I was told I had to take a Civil Service test which was scheduled for the following Monday. At that time, Monday meant only one thing to me - laundry. As I walked down the corridors of the University toward the personnel department, I thought to myself, "I wish I were home right now," even though I was never too keen on washing clothes. Nothing at that moment would have given me a more secure feeling than to be in my basement, facing a tub of hot sudsy water and a few piles of dirty laundry.

Before the tests began, I filled out a number of forms regarding my education and working experiences which I could have answered with one simple word, "limited."

After having filled in all the required questions, I started the second phase of the test

17

which consisted of some math problems, word association, finger dexterity, and other tests that I have blocked from my consciousness in the ensuing years.

When I finally completed the tests, I was told to wait in the corridor for the results. Some time passed, and finally, a man came out of an office and walked over to me. In a voice that I thought was exceptionally loud, he said, "Mrs. Kennedy, you've passed your tests, but you don't know how to do anything."

I don't remember the answer I gave to that remark, if any. All I remember is the embarrassment I felt. My first thought was, "How can I tell my family that I can't get a job because I don't know how to *do* anything?" Then I heard him say, "We do have a part-time job at Nicholson Hall Bookstore." Although it was for only two weeks out of each quarter, I jumped at the opportunity. I finally had a job! Later, I found out that because it was part-time, the job didn't require a Civil Service test. To work at Nicholson Hall Bookstore, I just had to be ambulatory.

Aside from the fact that the job was far from challenging, it didn't provide me with an adequate income. For the extra money I needed, I worked for my friends; work I was capable of doing, like washing walls, painting, refinishing furniture, house cleaning and ironing. Needless to say, some of these jobs did very little for my self-esteem.

In the past, when I had youth on my side, I used to think that someday I would be rich. The day would come when I wouldn't have to scrimp. I finally got to the point where it was a luxury to have napkins, paper towels, toilet tissue and kleenex all at the same time.

People frequently make the statement: "Money won't buy happiness." Maybe not directly, but it puts bread on the table, pays the mortgage, and pays for a tank full of oil. During the long harsh Minnesota winters, being warm made us all happy.

I remember one occasion when I called the oil company I had dealt with over the years and ordered a tankful of oil. The man on the other end of the line must have done a quick credit check, because he came back with, "That'll have to be C.O.D., Mrs. Kennedy." I hung up the phone and called him "a bastard." My girls heard me and were shocked at my outburst. They had never heard me swear before except, perhaps, for an occasional, "Hell, damn, spit." I apologized to them, but I felt good about it until I thought of the money I had to come up with to pay for the tank of oil. I was beginning to feel like Mrs. Wiggs in the Cabbage Patch.

19

In the past, I had found that when things really became difficult, something always presented itself. However, I always looked to others for the solution to my problems, not realizing that I had within myself powerful resources to solve my own problems and change my own conditions. This revelation didn't come to me in a blinding flash, but as the result of extensive reading of self-help books.

Today, unlike the past, there isn't a woman's magazine that doesn't deal with such problems as divorce, guilt, fear, loneliness and self-esteem. When I was trying to change my circumstances, I resorted to reading self-help books geared strictly for men, although, at the time, I didn't feel intimidated. I just mentally changed all the he's to she's.

As I began to read, I knew that here was a philosophy that made sense to me. I was aware of a feeling of knowing that I was finally on to something that was going to make a difference in my life. I read and reread, and found that I was discovering another self, a part of me which had always been there, another self that was encased in a hard shell of a low self-image.

As a result of all this reading, I finally realized that I could become the kind of person I wanted to be, to have what I wanted and needed, and to do what I wanted to do.

I developed a feeling of security. My security came from the knowledge that I had the ability to deal with my life and not depend on a promise from someone else. No one else was as concerned with my life as I was, and no one else could take the gamble out of my life for me. I had set up limitations in my mind, and it was in my mind that I began to change those limitations and reshape my life into what I wished it to be.

One year and many self-help books later, I again asked myself the same question, "What can I do?" This time, when my experiences as a model surfaced in my mind, instead of the thought "Who'd want me?", something had changed. I felt differently about myself. I could now say, "Why not me?" What a glorious feeling! I took a second look at my experience in modeling, and it didn't seem ridiculous to try to get back into fashion.

For the first time I knew in my heart, I could do it. I called for an appointment at one of the leading department stores and was given an appointment for a job interview for the following month. From that point until the day of the interview, I visualized the interview in my mind.

Each night after I went to bed, I would completely relax, then picture myself in an interview with the fashion director. By the end of the month, I felt very comfortable after twenty-four

21

The distance between the kitchen and the business world can be a million miles or it can be one giant step.

(imaginary) interviews.

Armed with a feeling of great expectation, a new self-image, and a two-piece dress exposing my knees for the first time in twenty years, I headed for my (real) fashion interview, which, due to my mental practicing, was an enjoyable experience rather than an ordeal.

At 2:30 in the afternoon of the same day, I received a call from the Fashion Director who told me that I was hired. I was now an assistant fashion coordinator.

From all of my experiences, I learned that the distance between the kitchen and a position in the business world can be a million miles or it can be one giant step, depending on our self-image. When we change our feelings about ourselves from "Who'd want me," to "Why not me?", we will have the confidence to check out the distance.

All of us have abilities we don't know about. We can do things we don't ever dream we can do. It's usually only when necessity forces us that we rise to the occasion and do the things that had seemed impossible before.

The knowledge that within us is the power to deal with anything that lies ahead makes an uncertain future a source of high adventure — instead of a drag.

"Make the most of yourself, for that is all there is of you."

RALPH WALDO EMERSON

What Can I Do For An Encore?

CHAPTER TWO

Today we have the means of attaining just about everything we set our minds to. Opportunities are all around us. In fact, there has never been a time when the world was as open to women as it is today.

Regardless of our position or circumstances, we can be in control of our lives. Anyone who desires to better their condition can do so. We only need one prerequisite — dissatisfaction. This doesn't mean dissatisfaction with husbands, children, employers, or friends. We need only to be dissatisfied with ourselves.

At the age of seventeen or eighteen, many of us reached a decision as to what we were going to do with our lives. Our future was decided upon by someone whose judgement we wouldn't even take into consideration today. (I shudder at the thought of my eighteen-year-old self making a decision today as to what I should do with the rest of my life.) And yet, many of us are *still* doing the things we decided to do at that time.

We complain about not knowing what we want to do today, or we make a decision that "the time isn't right," or "I'm not as young as I used to be." If we were honest with ourselves, we would have to admit that we are not making decisions but excuses. We build a wall of protection around us with our excuses. When one dissolves, we find another to take its place. This is one of the reasons why there are so many of us who are unhappy, frustrated, aimless and bored. Life is not interesting or fulfilling because we haven't committed ourselves to anything beyond our daily needs. Our conversation is laced with: "I should have," "Why didn't I," "I was supposed to."

As the years pass, we grow accustomed to the compromises we made with ourselves. We put away the dreams we once had, and we no longer want to think of them because they seem ridiculous today.

We stay in the same job year after year, or we continue to stay at home, even though many of our responsibilities have completely evaporated. Many of us slip from youth to middle age with a vague feeling that we want something more out of life, yet we make little effort to find out what it is. We hold with F. Scott Fitzgerald that, *"There are no second acts in America."*

At a certain age, we feel that we have neither the time nor energy to make any changes or plans for the future. We hesitate to take up anything new, especially if it will cover an extended period. We accept the fact that we are too old to even make an attempt, and we let it go at that.

At age forty or fifty, we begin to let down. A backache, which would have gone unnoticed earlier in our life, is now accepted as a mark of age. We are vulnerable to the remarks of our family and friends. We are told not to do this or that because we aren't as young as we used to be. Self-pity becomes our biggest indoor sport.

If we accept the fact that being forty, fifty, or sixty is old, then we accept the fact that we have reached an age where we can no longer grow. We have to assume that what we have achieved is all that we can hope to achieve, and from now on it's all downhill.

That is not the way it has to be for any of us. There is an enormous amount of research to show that we are capable of functioning beautifully, not only productively, intellectually, but also sexually, well into our eighties. We create our own age consciousness.

Self-pity becomes
our biggest indoor sport.

We make the mistake of listening to our neighbors, relatives and friends, rather than listening to our own instincts. We should stop listening to others in matters where only we may have the answers that pertain to our lives.

I received a letter from a woman who said,

"At times I'm up and at times I'm down. I've had to battle against insecure feelings all my life. Now I know I had put too much faith in people who put me down or made me feel I wasn't worth much. I know that if I try and want to, I can accomplish things. I'm sorry that it has taken thirty-seven years for me to get my act together."

In giving self-improvement seminars to women around the country, I usually hand out a simple evaluation form. Some of the questions I ask are:

How do you feel about yourself?

What are some of the things you say about yourself?

The answers that are most frequently given are:

"I'm not very bright"

"I'm unattractive"

"I procrastinate"

"I can't do anything but housework"

"I don't do anything right"

"I'm getting old"

"I don't have confidence in myself"

31

Psychologists define an inferiority complex as an emotional state in which a person feels he or she cannot achieve success because of imaginary deficiencies. This sense of inferiority produces very real emotions, such as the lack of confidence, insecurity, and a feeling of incompetence.

Many share these feelings. The feeling of inferiority is perhaps our greatest handicap. It is not necessarily confined to specific situations, but from time to time we are burdened by a general sense of our unfitness. The basic problem is that we are so familiar with ourselves that we tend to take ourselves for granted.

We all change over the years, but what often does not change is our inhibitions which we've dragged around with us since we were young. After years of living, we can see new strengths, yet our attitude toward ourselves has not been updated.

Through force of habit, we pinpoint an overwhelming number of inadequacies. On the other hand, we minimize those strengths which can be to our advantage in the business world.

We make a habit of comparing ourselves to others, and invariably we come out second best. The fallacy lies in the fact that we compare our weaknesses with their strengths. In the course of a day we might meet someone who is smarter, more attractive, thinner, younger, a better cook, a better mother, a better homemaker, a better tennis player, a better golfer — always someone who is more talented, more organized, someone who can do things better than we can. The list is endless. No wonder we feel as we do.

With this attitude of inferiority, we are prone to fill our thoughts with remorse and regrets. We are disappointed in ourselves and with our accomplishments.

I received a letter from a woman who wrote: "I am a homemaker with two children, a good husband who works hard. I have everything to be happy about, but it doesn't seem enough. Before I had children, I was a very confident hairdresser. I loved doing things for people. It was fun doing something creative, and making others look good at the same time.

"Now I've become a bore, dependent on my husband for too many things. I know inside of me somewhere there is that other independent, confident person. I would just like to get her out.

"A confident, well established man like my husband could never understand, and those, who do, like my friends, are either afraid to admit that they feel the same way, or couldn't help anyway.

"I have a little part-time job, but it is a bore. My bosses are all younger than myself and they act as if they are the knowledgeable superiors. I don't begrudge them their position, but I feel that at thirty-five years of age, I am back to the position I was when I was sixteen years old.

"Aside from working part-time, I do some of my husband's paper work, take care of the children, clean the house, cook etc . . . It's just a thankless merry-go-round."

One of the most difficult things in life to achieve is recognizing our own individual identity. We all need to feel that we are important, but we need to feel that other people *recognize* this importance. We need this recognition to establish our sense of personal worth. Many of us are living frustrated lives because we take a doubtful attitude toward ourselves and, as a result, toward life in general.

Our position in life is not the result of inferior abilities, but of the inferior opinion we have of ourselves. We exaggerate the extent of our inferiority to the point that we expand it to matters in which we really are not inferior, and consequently we let it cloud our vision and hold us back from the accomplishments that are well within our reach. When our self-image is low we

34

tend to stay with the familiar, the routine. We have a fear of new challenges.

Before real changes can take place in our lives, we must search within ourselves, become aware of who we are and what is possible. We will never know who we "really" are until we deal with the person we "think" we are.

It is an accepted fact that the limitations we feel, the goals we set for ourselves, our whole attitudes toward life, are strongly influenced by the image we have of ourselves.

Our inner self creates our limitations. We can control the direction of our lives, but an inadequate self-image limits us from achieving our potential. Many of the beliefs we hold about ourselves today stem from our experiences as children.

Some of us burden ourselves with a false humility. We have belittled ourselves so much and have come to accept ourselves as so worthless that we have decided the only way we can ever get any of the acceptance we need from others is to be subservient.

When I was twelve years old, I was given the opportunity of going to a Girl Scout camp. Aside from the learning experiences and the fun we had at Camp Lagamaga, we all had daily duties to perform. One of the most unpopular of these was cleaning the latrine. When it was my turn, I did it and didn't think anything of it. The following day, one of the girls approached me and asked if I would clean the latrine for her. She was the governor's daughter, which impressed me. I wanted her to be my friend, so I cleaned it for her. The next day, another girl approached me and asked the same question. So I cleaned it again. The word must have spread throughout the camp, because I found myself with the steady job of cleaning the latrine.

It was many years and many experiences later that I learned a basic fact of life, "If you don't want to be walked on, get off the floor, because when you're down there, someone is bound to step on you."

We set the value that others place on us. If we under-rate ourselves, others are likely to do the same.

In George Bernard Shaw's *Pygmalion,* Eliza Doolittle explains:

"You see, really and truly, apart from the things anyone can pick up (the dressing and the proper way of speaking and so on), the difference between a lady and a flower girl is not how she behaves, but how she's treated. I shall always be a flower girl to Professor Higgens, because he always treats me as a flower girl, and always will; but I know I can be

a lady to you, because you always treat me as a lady, and always will."

On the other hand, Anna Eleanor Roosevelt said, *"No one can make you feel inferior without your consent."*

There are things we can do without in our life, but the one thing we must have is a feeling of self-respect.

The ability to be successful is within all of us, but we put it from us each time we say:

"I'm not good enough"

"I'm afraid"

"Nothing seems to work out for me"

"Everything happens to me"

"I'm not bright"

"I can't"

To change things in our lives is a matter of changing our beliefs about them, whether about ourselves or our conditions.

We cannot achieve success in life if we constantly believe ourselves unworthy of it. We need to clean house and get rid of the ideas that diminish us as an individual. We have to start building a new concept, a new mental picture of the kind of person we would like to be.

We can begin to acquire a good self-image when we accept our imperfections as well as our perfections, for that's what we are, a combination of strengths and weaknesses. We should not

We set the value
that others place on us.

pretend to be anything other than what we are, because there is no other person on this earth who feels, acts, or thinks exactly as we do. We should not apologize for being who we are.

Creating a new self-image will release our talents and abilities. With a high regard for ourselves, not only will we feel more confident, but we will feel free to be ourselves and to express ourselves.

In another letter, a woman told me that she went back to nursing school at the age of forty-seven. She said,

"Since that time I feel good about myself. Previous to that time I was home, married to a man who is quite prominent in our community, and felt like a non-entity. So when the children were grown and educated, I educated myself with money I earned.

"I would advise any woman who has a poor self-image, and feels down, to get going; get out, and do something for herself if she has the health to do so. I have one regret. I should have done it sooner."

We are never too old to change. Within us is the ability and the power to do what we want to do. This power becomes available to us as soon as we change the beliefs we have about ourselves, as soon as we can rid ourselves of the ideas that "I can't," "I'm not good enough," and as soon as we tell ourselves "I can."

There is scientific proof that the creative energy of the mind and body are affected by our words and thoughts.

For years doctors have used the mind to cure patients. They gave them a pill called a placebo. A placebo is a nothing pill. It comes in a brightly colored capsule, and all it contains is a harmless white powder. When doctors prescribe it, with confidence and authority, it often produces remarkable recoveries. It can be effective because it can change the thinking of the patient. When a person's thoughts are changed, the condition of the body can be changed.

Words can also be used as a placebo.

If we don't have the things we want in life, if we aren't the person we would like to be, then we must look to our thoughts and the words we use when talking to others.

It is essential that we consciously discard negative phrases such as, "I don't have the confidence," "I don't know how to do anything," "Nothing is working out for me." Each negative thought and word brings upon us the very opposite of what we want.

Success, happiness and a great future are all around us and can be ours, depending on what we think and say each day.

40

Any of us, whether married, single, divorced or widowed, can have a more stimulating life, when we realize that there is more to us than meets the eye. With this awareness, we'll be on our way to exciting changes that only we can bring about, changes that are necessary for our mental and emotional well-being.

We cannot look to others to make our life more than it is. We have to live and grow within ourselves, and any changes in ourselves must involve changing our thinking.

> **"The Universe
> is change;
> our life
> is what
> our thoughts
> make it."**

MARCUS AURELIUS ANTONINUS

As A Woman Thinketh

CHAPTER THREE

The law of thought is as definite as other laws of nature. When we understand that happiness, health, success and other conditions are results, and that these results are created by positive thinking, we will realize the importance of controlling our thoughts.

Most of us believe that thoughts are invisible, yet we mark the existence of thousands of them visually each day.

Our thoughts are written on our faces, in the expression of our eyes, in the set of our lips, our posture, in the tone of our conversation, in our character, our successes and our failures.

We can't avoid the responsibility of what we experience in our daily life, for all experience is largely the result of our own thinking. Things happen in our mind before they can happen in our life. The conditions under which we live are a result of our thought process. An honest inventory of what we have in our everyday life will give us a good idea of the kind of thinking we have engaged in in the past and what has been impressed on our mind.

There are certain conditions we all desire for ourselves — to be happy, to be successful, to be satisfied with the life we are living, and to live it in the best possible manner. The problem is that we think negatively and hope for positive results.

Down through the centuries teachers and philosophers have told us about the effects of thought upon ourselves and our circumstances. Buddha said, *"What you think, you become."* The Book of Proverbs states, *"As a man thinketh in his heart, so is he."* The writings of the Upanishads say, *"As one's thinking is, such one becomes."*

These are simple words. They were not meant to confuse us, but to be pondered upon because of their tremendous power. Through these words we realize that thought is a vital living force that can mold and shape our lives. They assure us of a life of hope, assurance that whatever we want to be or achieve is possible.

More recently, William James, the Harvard psychologist, said, *"The greatest revolution in our generation is the discovery that human beings, by changing the inner attitude of their minds, can change the outer aspects of their lives."*

Once we are aware of the creative nature of thought, we will realize that what we are experiencing in our conditions, circumstances, and relationships is due to a consistent thought pattern.

To change the quality of our lives, we must change the quality of our thinking, become aware of the things we think about.

It isn't, however, the profound thought that we entertain in the course of our day that has an effect upon us, but the little repetitious thoughts that we have as we go about our daily lives.

A report issued in 1973 by the National Institute of Mental Health stated that 125,000 Americans are hospitalized with depression annually. Another 200,000 seek treatment for depression. Aside from these, it is estimated that another 4 to 8 million may need help, but are not aware of it. The report went on to say that outside of a traumatic experience, much of depression comes from wrong thinking; how people talk to themselves.

We have the option of choosing what we think, and, having done so, nothing can stop our decision from becoming a reality. No one willingly engages in negative and destructive thoughts or feelings; it's usually a pattern we have set unconsciously. Each negative thought that is impressed in our mind, however, brings

Thought is the most dynamic,
most creative element we
have to work with.

us the very opposite of what we really want.

If we were to review the thoughts we entertained or the emotions we felt today, would we want each one imprinted on our mind? Could we use every suggestion to further our purpose, or would half of our day's thoughts and emotions balance the other half, positive and negative, so that tonight we are no further ahead than we were yesterday?

Thought is the most dynamic, most creative element we have to work with. If it is not controlled, it can be the most destructive force in our lives.

An example of negative thinking appeared several years ago in a midwest newspaper headlined, "Woman Who Considered Herself A 'Bad Seed' Convicted in Slaying." The article stated that a woman had been found guilty of manslaughter slightly more than twenty-two years after her father was found guilty of a similar charge. In the years since her father's conviction, she had consistently referred to herself as the "bad seed."

In the book, "As a Man Thinketh," James Allen wrote, *"You are what you think, you attract what you think, your life is a product of your thoughts and beliefs, and nothing in the world can change this fact. To alter your life, the only course open to you is to alter your thinking."*

There is no one who can prevent us from being successful except ourselves. Whatever thoughts, attitudes, or opinions we impress on our mind, will be experienced in our life.

We can say, "This is how I feel," or "This is what I believe," but it is our deep-seated emotional convictions that will surface in our lives.

For example, a woman is reading the classified section in the newspaper which tells of an opportunity for a mature woman who is bright, ambitious and has the ability to communicate. Jane is fifty-two years old and not satisfied with her present job. She thinks about the ad for a few minutes, and then decides that they are probably looking for someone with more experience and more ability than she has and there is no point in answering the ad.

When we tell ourselves that we can't do something, then we either don't make an attempt, or we make a half-hearted attempt and tell ourselves that we knew all along that we couldn't do it.

In considering our future, we must only be concerned with the belief we have in it. If we *believe* we have no talents, if we *believe* we are too old, if we *believe* nobody wants us, these become our convictions, to be accepted by our mind and acted upon.

The important step toward a successful life is

the feeling that we can succeed. If we expect to fail, chances are we will. Our belief that we will succeed improves the possibility of success.

When we are confident, we will unconsciously do the necessary things that will bring success.

There are two methods by which we can change ourselves and our life. First, by affirmation, and secondly by utilizing our creative imagination.

Emil Coue, a French pharmacist living during the early part of this century, was considered a great authority on the power of suggestion. He astonished the world with the medical results he obtained through the power of suggestion as opposed to the ingestion of pills and syrups requested by his clientele. His suggestion, a simple affirmation *"Every day in every way I am getting better and better"* helped thousands in France as well as throughout the world.

It stands to reason that, if our present situation is the result of negative suggestions we have given our mind in the past, such as, "I don't have any confidence," "I'm disorganized," "I can't do anything right," the reverse can also come about. We fail through negative persistence and repetition; we can achieve by positive affirmation.

Prior to learning about the power of suggestion, I had always said to myself and others in conversation, "I'm afraid to stand up and speak

The important step toward
a successful life is the feeling
that we can succeed. If we
expect to fail, chances are
we will.

in front of people." I said it because it was a fact. The fear of public speaking had been with me for as long as I can remember. Each time I had to give a report or stand up and say anything other than my name in front of a group of people, my hands shook, my heart felt as though it had enlarged to twice its normal size, and began pounding wildly.

Once I realized that I had created this fear through years of negative suggestion of fear and nervousness, I stopped making the statement. Instead of using the word "afraid", I used the word "enjoy". I repeated the affirmation, "I thoroughly enjoy public speaking," five times each day. Slowly, I noticed a change. It became easier for me to stand up before a group of people and speak. Today I no longer have to cope with the paralyzing fear of public speaking. In fact, today I do the one thing I feared for so long. I speak to groups around the country, and I enjoy it.

Through affirmations, we can build up our self-image and achieve our goals. By the use of affirmations, it is possible to break old habits and replace them with new ones.

According to experts in the field of psychology, it takes about 21 days to break a habit or to form a new one.

We all experience the frustration of trying to adjust to simple changes we make in our home.

For example, I had two drawers in my kitchen that I decided to change. One was my silverware drawer, and the other was my junk drawer. One day, after having these drawers in the same place for over four years, I put the silverware in the junk drawer, which was close to the dinette and put the junk into the drawer that once held the silverware. I really thought I would expedite things immediately. As it turned out, it took me about a month to go to the right drawer when I needed something. Until then, I opened the junk drawer when I wanted to set the table, and I went to the silverware drawer when I wanted a pencil or screwdriver.

Because habits have the tenacity of an ant, it takes persistence and repetition to break them.

After the decision is made to break a habit or make a change, refrain from expressing doubt, difficulty, or the possibility of a negative outcome. Many of us on a diet will say, "It's so hard to stick to a diet." "I find myself always thinking of food." The fact that we make the statement leads to thoughts of food and we'll always be hungry. It's self-fulfilling prophesy.

Our behavior is largely determined by the words we use. We think in "words", and we tend to be governed by the words used in talking to ourselves mentally. If we want to make progress in raising our self-image or achieve our goals we must use positive words.

This is not something we should do on a part-time basis, neither is it a Pollyanna attitude. In order for us to make changes in ourselves and in our lives, we must use our tongue in a constructive manner.

The mind is extremely receptive, and can be convinced of any premise we present it, whether it is true or false, positive or negative. Through affirmations, we can stop smoking, lose weight, or get over an unhappy love affair. The first thing is to say, "I no longer need cigarettes in my life," and stop saying we "enjoy" them. "I no longer need (name of person) in my life." The words we use can be simple. But, if the effects are to be permanent, the affirmation must be continued until the desired results are obtained.

Affirmations should always be phrased with the final results we wish to achieve; for example, "I like and accept myself," rather than "I'm going to like and accept myself." "I'm well organized," rather than "I'm going to get organized." Affirmation must not be conditional.

Our future "nows" make us become the person we want to be, for this moment in time is our point of power wherein we can change our life by changing our beliefs about ourselves. This present moment - NOW - is the instant in time when we can make changes. We can't change yesterday. We can't make changes in the future.

There is only this moment, this now, that exists for us.

Our ambitions reflect the quality of our self-image. It is vital, therefore, that we begin making changes in this area. Some affirmations to raise our self-image are:

"I like and accept myself."

"I am completely relaxed and self-assured in all situations." "I am totally alive as a result of my positive thoughts and actions."

Forming visual images that associate with the affirmations are effective. In the first affirmation, "I like and accept myself," we should picture a time when we were good to someone, relive it, feel good about it. As we affirm we continue to visualize that experience, repeating each affirmation, slowly, five times.

To affirm is to state *it is so,* and, as we maintain this attitude of mind as true, regardless of all evidence to the contrary, we will gradually change.

When ready to make your affirmations, sit in a comfortable chair and relax your body. Start with your forehead, then work down to your shoulders, stomach, thighs, calves and feet. When you are completely relaxed, begin your affirmations.

Affirmations are a simple and effective way of bringing wonderful changes to ourselves and to our lives. Following a method of daily affirmations for even a short time will produce satisfying results.

In addition to using affirmations to make changes, we should utilize our creative imagination. The mind is a powerful tool, and it is within our power to *imagine* being a success, to *imagine* we are what we want to be. Imagination is not dreaming or fantasy. It is creating a real situation, one in the future, and thinking and seeing ourselves in that situation, whether in the performance of some particular task or as actually occupying the position to which we aspire.

It is necessary for us to have a clearly defined image in our mind of ourselves as we desire to be. We must see ourselves attracting good things by the power of our mental forces. What we create in this manner, in our mind, will later be relived in our lives.

We must picture what we really want, not just what we think we can probably have. If we give our imagination half-hearted mental pictures, that's the kind of results we'll get.

The most important ingredient in the achievement of success is self-confidence. Without this characteristic, our chances of demanding more from life or broadening our horizons are pretty dismal. With self-confidence, we have the courage to take chances which success demands of us. Each time we experience a success, it instills further self-confidence which

57

in turn breeds more confidence.

But, how do we feel confident when we haven't felt confident in years? In his book, "Psycho Cybernetics," Dr. Maxwell Maltz gives us the answer. He said, *"Mental pictures offer us an opportunity to "practice" new traits and attitudes, which otherwise we could not do. This is possible because your nervous system cannot tell the difference between an actual experience and one that is vividly imagined."*

Years ago, Shakespeare expressed the same thought when he said, *"Assume a virtue if you have it not."*

Night-time is ideal to give full reign to our imagination, when we are in bed and in a relaxed position - imagining how it would feel as the kind of person we would like to be, to see ourselves among people, no longer shy, but moving with ease, and feeling good about it - to see ourselves in a past situation, formerly anxious and fearful, but now acting calmly, feeling confident. We can also recall and visualize in detail experiences from the past, in which we moved with confidence and achieved success. See the incident clearly in our mind. Recall the people who were a part of the experience. Remember how they looked, what they said, and how we felt during the experience. Become again, in our imagination, the person we were at that time. Repeat this process, using one or several successful experiences. The more we relive successful past happenings, the more confidence we are building within ourselves.

When we have achieved a feeling of confidence, through affirmation and the use of our creative imagination, we will notice a change in the attitude of the people around us. With confidence, we will become relaxed, more assertive and enjoy life more. We will no longer feel intimidated at every turn.

For these methods to be successful, however, it is necessary for us to believe that results will follow. If we do, we can expect our life to change in many ways.

What happens tomorrow is but the shadow of thoughts we held today.

TECHNIQUE FOR PHYSICAL RELAXATION

1. Close your eyes.

2. Breath slowly, deeply, and rhythmically.

3. Tense the muscles of your face and relax. Repeat the same tensing and relaxing from your face to your neck, to your arms, hands, finger, abdomen, legs, and feet.

4. Let your whole body relax.

TECHNIQUE FOR MENTAL RELAXATION

1. After about a minute in the physical relaxation exercise, take a deep breath and slowly exhale.

2. Now see yourself in the successful role you have always desired. Keep this picture in your mind for about two minutes.

3. Open your eyes and stretch your whole body.

This exercise can also be used for your affirmations. When using this relaxation technique, it should be performed in a sitting position in a quiet and comfortable area.

SUGGESTED AFFIRMATIONS

Affirmations For Personal Growth

"I have an excellent memory."

"I am well organized in all areas of my life."

"I am persistent. I finish each project I begin."

"I am truthful with myself and others."

"I am becoming more understanding of others."

"I enjoy learning ....(Name subject).

Affirmations For Better Health

"I am easily able to relax."

"I have a tremendous amount of energy."

"I get along very well without smoking."

"I do not need alcohol in my life."

"I enjoy being on my diet."

**"If we did
all the things
we are capable
of doing,
we would literally
astound
ourselves."**

THOMAS A. EDISON

Reach
Out
For
More

CHAPTER FOUR

We all have our own idea of what success means. To some it means money or position. To others, it may mean knowledge. Whatever we consider success to be, we can achieve if we are willing to make it the deep desire of our life.

The most important question we can ever ask ourselves is, "What do I want to do in my life above everything else?" Whether the answer to that question is a career, avocation, a business, or helping others, is our decision alone.

It is vital that we have something to strive for, something in the back of our mind that we want, something to be accomplished. Setting goals:
- helps us discover what we really want to do.
- gives purpose to the way we spend our time.
- motivates us.
- gives direction to our lives.

We all have planned for a vacation, knowing exactly where we're going, how we will travel, and what it will cost. Few would ever waste time driving around aimlessly until our vacation time was up. Yet so many of us do just that with our life. We haven't set a course because we haven't determined our destination.

In the three stages of life, childhood, young adult, and maturity, the third plateau is recognized today as the period where people really grow. It is a time to realize that we can no longer wait to decide if we are achieving our life-long goals, and to evaluate what we have done and what we want to do.

Life holds no real success until we find that which fulfills us. To not find it is to lose time, and each birthday only serves as a reminder of lost opportunities.

During one conversation a woman said to me, "The years are rushing by all of a sudden, and I'm in a hurry to do everything because I'm forty. I look back and I realize I haven't done anything that I was going to do when I was eighteen or twenty. I spent years raising children. Everything I've ever done falls into that category. I know I wanted to set goals, but I didn't, I just went along. I thought, "next week - next month - next year," and now I'm looking back at those years and I haven't accomplished any of those goals."

To gain control over our lives, we must have a basic plan rather than just letting it happen. One of the most important benefits derived from setting a goal and planning how to achieve it is that great feeling of expectancy that occurs when we know "something" is happening in our lives, and we are making it happen.

Once we realize the part thoughts and desires play in our daily life, we must decide *what* we desire.

If we are to achieve more than we presently have, we must start with a desire, for living successfully, getting the things we want from life, is a matter of solving the problems which stand between where we are now and where we want to be. When we are trying to find the answer to the question, "What am I going to do?" "What can I do?", we must look to something other than our conscious mind for the answer.

Thomas Paine, in referring to the source of his great storehouse of knowledge, said,

"Any person who has made observation on the state of progress of the human mind by observing his own, cannot but have observed that there are two distinct classes of what are called thoughts: Those that we produce in ourselves by reflection and the act of thinking, and those that bolt into the mind of their own accord."

67

> **To gain control over our lives,**
> **we must have a basic plan**
> **rather than just**
> **letting it happen.**

The first step in solving our problems is to define them.

1. Write down the problem on a sheet of paper.
2. Gather information regarding the problem.
   a. Our own information.
   b. Information we can get from others.
3. Work the problem out on paper. (Pros and cons)
4. If the solution doesn't present itself, we should turn it over to our subconscious mind.
5. Then get busy with some other activity.

It is necessary to have a firm conviction that results will follow.

Each of us has had the experience of trying to find the solution to a perplexing problem. When we finally ignored it, or focused on some other activity, the solution suddenly flashed into our mind.

A simple example of how our subconscious mind helps us solve problems becomes clear to us when we forget a name. We try consciously to recall it, but when we finally give up trying, the name surfaces.

If we want our subconscious mind to come up with a solution, we must give it something to work on. By listing the things we enjoy doing in our spare time, do naturally, plus things we have accomplished in our life, we give our subconscious mind facts to work on. This list will also provide us with two benefits: first, self-esteem and good feelings about ourselves, from reviewing past achievements and strengths, and second, we begin to see that we have talents and skills we were not aware of.

When we give our subconscious mind a problem to solve, one that we have consciously worked on for some time, our mind will accept it, work on it, and give us back the solution.

Once we know what we want to do, there are many ways of obtaining outside information that can help us achieve our objective. We can inquire about educational opportunities available in many adult programs in universities and high schools. We can acquire knowledge. We can learn from the experiences of others. We can ask people who have already succeeded how they got where they are today. Pertinent questions: What was your first job? How did you get it? Where did you go from there? Most people are willing to tell of their experiences.

Look around for women who are making the most of their lives, famous women, or women in your community or social circle. Note how they dress, their manner, their lifestyle. We all need a model or image to emulate. Reading biographies of famous women, for instance, points up characteristics that made them great.

Many of us have been so intimidated and immobilized by feelings of inadequacy that we are willing to settle for less than we desire. We live uncreative lives while all the time possessing the ability and resources to achieve more.

Many of us are hesitant as to how high we should reach. Our belief in ourselves is the measurement.

Here is an impressive and delightful story told to me by a woman who now owns her own kosher catering business, and how she accomplished it.

"I decided to go into business five years ago. My children started school, and I was home alone. I hate house work. I thought, 'I would rather go out and work and have, someone else come in and clean my house.'

"My only qualification was teaching elementary school. Now, I had just sent my children off to school, and I really didn't want to spend the day with twenty-six other children. The only other thing I could do was cook. I enjoy cooking for a large group, making all the fancy dishes and beautiful desserts. As a result, instead of doing the housework, I had large costly parties simply to keep occupied.

71

"People started calling and asking if I would help them. I thought that was wonderful, because now it would be their expense not ours. After a while, I was doing so much work on their parties, it was ridiculous. I became so involved with it I decided, if I'm going to do it, it might as well pay. That's when I decided to become a caterer.

"I was in business a very short time when I realized that the only way to make it profitable was to become a kosher caterer, catering in the temples because these people could not go to a fancy restaurant and get it kosher. There was a need for this type of business.

"I went to Boston to get a license. Being a kosher caterer is probably one of the most difficult things to accomplish. They are ultra-strict. You are governed by the dietary laws, which for many years were health laws. Things have progressed over the years, but you still must abide by them because the rabbis say you must. They feel they are necessary. They are part of the religion and people live by them. If you are going to cater to these people, you must also abide by these dietary laws.

"I went before a board of twenty-five rabbis and the first things they said were, 'This shouldn't be a business for a nice little girl like you. You don't want to be involved in this. You don't need this aggravation.'

"Well, I sat there and I decided as I looked at them, 'I'm going to do it and sooner or later you are going to give me a license.' They could have discouraged me twenty years ago. I would have been willing to forget the whole thing, figuring, 'Oh well, I'll find something else to do.' Here was this board of rabbis speaking Hebrew to each other, which I don't understand. I was sitting there trying to get my point across and all I heard from them was, 'This is a very hard business. This is a man's work. This is a man's thing. Go home, take care of your husband and your children.' I sat there and they told me I couldn't do it because I am a woman.

"When I got back home, I went to see my rabbi. I asked him if he would go before the board with me. He could talk to them because he speaks Hebrew. I told him I didn't understand what they were saying. We went back and, through him, I got my point across. They gave me a conditional license for six months. They wanted to watch me. They were extremely careful to make sure that I followed every rule that they set forth. I really enjoyed doing it, and I didn't find it that difficult. I was brought up in a kosher home so I knew basically what they were talking about.

73

"We went six months on a dairy license. They would not allow me to handle meat at all because it was more complicated. But I discovered in six months that there wasn't any money in dairy. The people who came to me were looking for the small, inexpensive type function, instead of weddings, for which they wanted roast beef.

"So, I went back to the board and told them I wanted to handle meat. To do this involved building another kitchen. You are not allowed to have dairy and meat kitchens on the same floor for fear that some of the utensils will be mixed together.

"I really had to assess the fact of whether or not to go on because it would be a very costly venture. My husband and I talked it over and he said, 'Go ahead.'

"Today, we have an extremely successful kosher catering business."

Studies show that individuals have a tendency to adopt society's evaluation of their capabilities. Until recently, society never expected women to succeed in businesses or the professions. Years of social conditioning have influenced women to establish more modest career goals than those set by men.

When we desire achievement we must know exactly what it is we want. We must have a deep desire for it. We must do everything we can to bring it about, and we must make up our mind that we are going to get it. But, we must be willing to pay the price, whether in time, effort, study, or money.

In the book, "The Knack of Using Your Subconscious Mind," John K. Williams wrote,

"You can, in very truth, have about whatever you want if you want it badly enough. But the world will give you nothing without extracting its price. By nature, as well as by the Law of the Universe, you cannot receive or be given something for nothing. That is not in the scheme of things. Take what you need and want. But pay for it you must, in one way or another.

The Universe is a great gambler. It seldom defines the price of anything with certainty. You must be willing to take a chance. Only one thing is certain: your desire sets the limit of your attainment, the price you are willing to pay is the measure of what you will get."

Many of us are not willing to commit ourselves to achieving our goal. We waste our time and talents working in jobs we dislike, or we stay home long after it is necessary. Each of these situations provides us with a safe haven.

Some of us have a secret wish and make a half-hearted attempt to fulfill it, but because our effort *is* half-hearted, we make excuses for ourselves by saying we didn't have the time, or circumstances weren't right to fulfill it. Maurice Chevalier said, *"If you wait for the perfect moment when all is safe and assured, mountains will not be climbed, races won, or lasting happiness achieved."*

If we acknowledge our goals as worth working for, and we focus our thoughts and energies on achieving them, our chances of making them a reality will increase.

It is a great day in our lives when we discover our latent abilities, many of which are greater than we realize.

Once we decide on a goal, one of our main problems may be the fear of criticism. There will be many people who won't be nearly as enthusiastic about our ambitions as we are. Our family and friends will give us a hundred reasons why we can't do what we want to do, and if we are not careful, we ourselves will think of a hundred more reasons.

We look to others for approval, for through approval we gain confidence. How many dreams have gone down the drain because we didn't get the needed approval from our family and friends? This need for approval can keep us from achieving our goal or missing an opportunity.

We also make a great mistake when we look

to others for advice about what we should or should not do. If we ourselves don't know, how can anyone else know? It is beneficial to ask for instructions and advice as to how to *do* a certain thing, but we should refrain from asking anyone *if* we should or not do it.

Many people insist upon looking for problems. In doing so, they affect those around them with their doom and gloom attitude.

An example of this comes from a story written in the Clarkson Letter. The title is, "How to Invite a Depression."

"A man lived by the side of the road and sold hot dogs. He was hard of hearing so he had no radio. He had trouble with his eyes so he read no newspapers. But he sold good hot dogs. He put up signs on the highway telling how good his hot dogs were. And people bought. He increased his meat and bun orders. He bought a bigger stove to take care of his trade. He got his son home from college to help him.

But then something happened. His son said, "Father, haven't you been listening to the radio? There's a depression on. The European situation is terrible. The domestic situation is worse."

Whereupon the father thought, "Well, my son's been to college. He reads the papers and he listens to the radio. And he ought to know."

So the father cut down on his meat and bun orders, took down his advertising signs, and no longer bothered to stand out on the highway to sell his hot dogs. And his hot dog sales fell almost overnight.

"You're right son," The father said to the boy. "We certainly are in the middle of a great depression."

A woman who attended one of my seminars told me that she wanted to go into business with her husband. They had a wonderful opportunity to buy a beauty shop, but they made the mistake of discussing it with their friends. Their friends comments were typical. "You've never had the experience of running a business." "There are too many beauty shops already." "The economy is bad." Only one of their friends said, "What have you got to lose?" Their final decision was not to go into business at that time.

She said, "We listened to everyone except the one person who said, 'What have you got to lose?' By not going ahead with our plans at that particular time, we missed our biggest opportunity."

We are constantly confronted with people who are tied to old beliefs and ideas. They are quick to tell us, "It can't be done," and, because we lack confidence in ourselves, we are easily convinced that it can't.

We all have moments when we see clearly how we can do certain things, but we don't believe in ourselves or them enough to make them a reality. Someone else will come along with no more ability or background than we have and do the very thing we had only *thought* of doing.

Fear and faith are the greatest factors competing for control of our mind, especially when we are thinking in terms of setting or achieving goals. Many of us have had negative experiences, experiences that hurt or disappointed us. These experiences can put doubts in our mind about our ability to succeed. Our tendency to focus on the negative aspects of life only helps to impress these negative things deeper in our mind.

Mark Twain said, *"We should be careful to get out of an experience only the wisdom that is in it - and stop there, lest we be like the cat that sits down on a hot stove lid. She will never sit down on a hot stove again - and that is well; but she also will never sit down on a cold one anymore."*

There is no philosophy that will help us to succeed if we doubt our ability to do so. No matter how hard we work for success, if our thoughts are filled with the fear of failure, they will paralyze our efforts.

To succeed in life, to do the things we want to

There is no philosophy that
will help us to succeed if we
doubt our ability to do so.

do, to have the things we want to have, our mind must focus steadily on what we *want*, not on what we don't have. Whatever our mind holds to is what we will have in our life.

Once we decide upon a goal, there are basic steps to follow to achieve our objectives:

1. *The Desire.* Desire is the motivating force in all of us. Without it, nothing can be achieved. We don't know the means by which the subconscious mind uses everything within reach to change our desires into reality. Desire is the starting point, and it is the foundation of achievement. To desire deeply is to have singleness of purpose.

2. *Put Goals In Writing.* Whatever we want should be written out as a clear statement of what we wish to achieve. The written statement provides a solid base from which to unlock that door between daydreams and reality. In the process of writing down our goals, we have made a commitment.

3. *Be Specific.* It is essential that we avoid general statements, such as "more money." Write the amount we desire. If our goal is a career, write down exactly what we want. If our goal is a house, the exact picture of the house will be effective. The mind needs a blueprint of our goals. The written words and pictures are our blueprints.

4. *Time Factor.* It is important to decide on

the length of time it will take to achieve our goal. If we fail to consider the time factor, it can cause us to give up too soon. It also gives us a sense of urgency.

5. *Refrain From Discussing Goals With Others.* Unless they include a special person or family, talking at length about our plans and goals can diminish our motivation. Sharing our plans with others also creates pressure for us to meet their expectations and makes it more difficult to change our mind. Also, talking about our plans may invite opinions that can inhibit us from taking action.

6. *Picture Goals.* Using our imagination to create a picture in our mind, and visualizing ourselves in the possession of our goal is important. If our goal is a particular job, we should see ourselves working in that position. If it's a place we want to visit, we should picture ourselves in that location. Our imagination is a part of our mind that plays a great role in achieving our goals.

Writing the goal on a 3x5 card will prove beneficial. We should read our goal first thing in the morning and the last thing at night. Through repetition we will impress our goal in our mind.

When we have our goal clearly defined, it is important to develop the feeling of expectations.

We set up our own limitations in our mind, and it is in our mind that we can begin changing those limitations.

Our reasoning power may indicate that it can never be, or our goal is too big to come true. But if we continue to imagine it anyway, then our creative imagination will go to work for us. Whatever the mind expects, that is what it will produce.

When we are willing to settle for left-overs, that's all we can expect to get. Second best should not be good enough for us.

Florence Chadwick was the first woman to swim the English channel in both directions. Her first attempt was on a foggy day, and she gave up just three miles short of the French coast. On her return to England, she said, "If I could have seen France, I would have made it." Her second try was on a clear sunny day and she succeeded.

The mind will always work for us. But we must give it a blueprint of the things we want. When we decide on the goal we want to achieve, we must develop the feeling of expectation.

William James said, *"If you want a quality, act as if you already had it."*

No one can stand in the way of a will that wants. Be positive — Be determined.

83

Strong positive expectations must be impressed in our mind. A dynamic and enjoyable way to create great expectations is the use of actual pictures. We can lay out our future in a scrapbook or loose-leaf notebook. These pictures should exemplify:

The person we want to become.

The home we wish to live in.

The car we want to drive.

The wardrobe we want to have.

The places we want to visit.

The position we want to achieve in our work.

The career we want to have.

To make this Goal Book effective, we should look through it each night upon retiring, and as many times as we can during the day. This is one way of developing a strong feeling of expectancy.

The important thing to remember is, not where we were in the past, or where we are today, but where we desire to be in the future.

A lovely man said:

> *The stars come nightly to*
> *the sky;*
> *The tidal wave unto*
> *the sea;*
> *Nor time, nor space, nor*
> *deep, nor high,*
> *Can keep my own away*
> *from me.*

John Burroughs

FOUR SPECIFIC AREAS
TO BE CONSIDERED:

BUSINESS AFFAIRS
1. A better Job
2. A career
3. A business of my own

FINANCIAL GOALS
1. A substantial bank account
2. A new automobile
3. A new home
4. Travel

MENTAL GOALS
1. Knowledge
2. Self-Improvement
3. Cultural
4. Building Confidence

PHYSICAL GOALS
1. Weight reduction
2. Quit smoking
3. Better health
4. More energy

NOTES

ACTION PLAN

When we decide on our major goal, we must determine our short range goals, for it is the achievement of our short range goals that will help us to finally arrive at our major objective. There's no point in knowing what we want if we don't have an action plan for it.

BUSINESS AFFAIRS

My long-range goal, for my business affairs, ___years from now. _____

My plans for achieving it:

1. _____

2. _____

3. _____

4. _____

My short range goal, for my business affairs, one year from now: _____

Things I will do each day to achieve it:

1. _____

2. _____

3. _____

4. _____

NOTES

FINANCIAL GOAL

My long-range financial goal,___ years from now._____

My plan for achieving it:

1._____
2._____
3._____
4._____

My short-range financial goal, one year from now._____

Things I will do each day to achieve it:

1._____
2._____
3._____
4._____

NOTES

MENTAL GOALS

My long-range mental goal,___years from now.

_____

My plan for achieving it:

1._____
2._____
3._____
4._____

My short-range mental goal, one year from now._____

Things I will do each day to improve myself mentally:

1._____
2._____
3._____
4._____

NOTES

PHYSICAL GOAL

My long-range physical goal,____years from now.
_____

My plan for achieving it:

1._____
2._____
3._____
4._____

My short-range physical goal, one year from now._____

Things I will do each day to achieve it:

1._____
2._____
3._____
4._____

94

"Procrastination is the art of keeping up with yesterday."

DONALD ROBERT PERRY MARQUIS

How
Many
More
Septembers?

CHAPTER FIVE

IN establishing our major goal, we set a course for our life, and also determine what we should do each day to achieve our objective.

Sometimes a goal will seem too far in the future. It seems that we'll never achieve it, and we might fall back into our old habits of time consumption. We may belong to several groups and organizations that expect us to give some of our time to committee work or meetings. We feel we must attend weddings, cocktail parties, luncheons. Unexpected interruptions also make demands on our time. People drop in. Telephone calls coupled with routine activities can prevent us from having extra time to pursue a major goal.

Until we learn to be selective in saying "yes", and comfortable with saying "no", we will not have the time and energy to do what we want to do. We get involved in activities or projects to please others, even when we don't really want to do it. If we can stop doing some of the things we don't want to do, we will find it much easier to say "yes" to activities that are really important to us. It is up to us to decide whether or not we want to eliminate some of the non-productive things we find the time to do.

In a recent newspaper article concerning a telephone conversation between a columnist and a well-known woman, the columnist wrote of her unsuccessful attempts to schedule a personal interview with this busy woman. During the telephone interview, the woman recounted her schedule, which consisted of jetting back and forth between New York and Europe, selling her house, redecorating an apartment, and a never-ending business and social calendar of appointments and events. When asked by the persistent columnist for "just" forty-five minutes, the super-busy woman exclaimed, "I won't have forty-five minutes until 1985."

Today everything moves fast, or so it seems. Sometimes the pressures we're under are the result of trying to do too many things in too short a time. We find ourselves saying:

"How can I possibly do everything I ought to do today?"

"The things I do aren't necessarily the things I want to do."

"I'm too busy to get things done."

I had a friend who was a classic example of a woman who had lots of time on her hands, but she didn't know it. She was too busy keeping her home spotless and organized.

She had an organizational plan for every room in her house. In the bathroom, she had boxes that she covered with contact paper. Each box was labeled by the contents, "Stomach Ailments," "Foot Ailments," and "Head Ailments." Every shelf in the bathroom closet was labeled and every toothbrush. But her labeling didn't end there. In the kitchen she emptied the contents from boxes into glass jars or cans that she also covered with contact paper and labeled each can. Years later, after she was in her own public relations business, she said, "Why would anyone want to cover a baking powder can, and label it "Baking Powder?"

"Once," she said, "I got up during the middle of the night and rearranged an entire wall of books." She said, "I was so frustrated and had to keep going. There couldn't be a corner of the house that wouldn't be perfect when I looked at it."

There is a vast number of women addicted to rearranging their furniture. We seem to have a

The first step in making changes is the decision to change.

compulsion to change our environment. In doing this, we divert our energies and leave
ourselves little time or motivation to pursue
what we should consider important.

Some time ago, I read a short story in a
magazine about a woman who was constantly
rearranging the furniture in her home. On one
occasion she decided to re-arrange the furniture
in the bedroom. That night her husband return-
ed home late from the office, and, not wanting to
disturb her, didn't bother to turn on the light in
the bedroom. As he went to get into bed, he fell
on the floor. The next day he took care of the
impossible situation — he nailed down all the
furniture in the house.

After 2,473 mornings of coffee klatching with
our neighbors or 74 attempts to find a new place
for the sofa, we come to a point where we ask
ourselves, "Is this all there is?"

The first step in making any changes is the
decision to change — to decide that we want
more out of life, that we want something else in
our lives. We must make the decision to
eliminate all the non-essential activities that we
have become involved with over the years, things
that fill up time and do nothing for us.

A recent survey on women who work outside
the home stated that, "A woman immediately
becomes more efficient at home and on the job.

She stops unnecessary tasks because there isn't time. Assignments for members of the family were given on a much more systematic basis and schedules were posted."

We will not get bogged down by our domestic obligations while we are handling two jobs, working toward our goals, or going to school, if we:

1. Plan each day.
2. Start each day a little earlier.
3. Delegate tasks. (Anyone over five.)
4. Shorten telephone calls. (Greatest time consumer.)
5. Eliminate all unproductive work.
6. Less rigid housekeeping habits.

The most important step is organization. We all have certain habits we continue to tolerate simply because they have *become* habits and are done automatically. For instance, most of us have a drawer in which we throw all our mail, notes to ourselves, recipes, notices of meetings, S&H green stamps, items clipped from magazines, coupons, pencils, paper clips and rubber bands.

When the time comes for us to answer a letter or pay a bill, we have no other alternative but to paw through the entire drawer until we find the letter or bill we want. It doesn't take an efficiency expert to point out that we are wasting time by continually searching for one thing or another. Buying a file box and fifteen or twenty manila folders would eliminate the big search. It is a waste of time to handle the same piece of paper over and over again, be it a letter, coupon, or magazine article. There are three things we can do with paper: deal with it, file it, or discard it.

A good way to get a clear perspective of how we spend our time from morning until night is to list all of our activities on a sheet of paper. By measuring time spent on these activities, we can determine how much time we waste on time-consuming, nonproductive activities, and how much time we are directing toward our highest priorities. List them as:

1. Daily routine activities. (daily tasks)
2. The non-productive things I do.
3. Record telephone calls.
4. Most productive tasks.

No matter how busy we feel we are, it is vital that we take the time to plan each day, for, if our goal is going to be reached in a minimum of time, every day must count.

Set priorities every day. Otherwise we'll get bogged down with activities that have little importance. The list can be made that morning or in the evening for the following day. There are certain routine tasks we all have which need not

103

be listed. The list should include tasks that might be put off if they were not written down. An important consideration in making out the list is that at least one task for the day should pertain to our goal. After the list is completed, number each task in order of their importance, then start with number one and stay with it until it is completed. If, for some reason, it cannot be completed, move on to number two.

Stay flexible, because there is always a possibility of some unforseen occurrence that can prevent us from following the exact plan for the day.

Our daily list is not etched in stone. If there are uncompleted tasks on our list by the end of the day, they can be added to the list for the following day in order of their importance for that day.

Write your list in a notebook or stenographer's pad. This will not only provide you with a record of what you have accomplished each day, but it's easier to keep tract of than a scrap of paper.

Much has been written about personal efficiency, general efficiency, and just about every other kind of efficiency. We all have to find what works best for each of us.

However, to simplify our lives we should:

- Know what it is we really want.
- Write it down.
- Analyze what we have to do to get it.
- Make a plan.
- Plan our activities for each day.
- Do one thing at a time.
- In this manner, we will become more confident with each passing day. We will assume control of our life. We will realize that the difference between our success and failure will hinge on whether we do something today or tomorrow, because a successful life is nothing more than a lot of successful days woven together.

"Success in life is a matter not so much of talent or opportunity as of concentration and perseverance."

C.W. WENDTE

Focus
on the
Objective

CHAPTER SIX

Achievement calls for three qualities:
1. The ability to make decisions
2. Persistence
3. Concentration
It is the possession of these qualities that separates the woman who *does* things from the woman who merely thinks about doing them; the woman of action, from the day-dreamer.

Each of us has had our inspirations, but have failed to follow them through, and here is where the danger lies. When we have the urge to do something, we must act.

We may have good intentions when we say we are "going to" do something, but "going to" can imply next week, next month, or next year. We need to change "going to" to "now."

The step doesn't have to be great, nothing

Ideas need life breathed
into them through definite
plans for immediate action.

more than a telephone call, or a letter written asking for information. In doing it *now* we have started.

We might have a project ahead of us about which we are not quite certain. Our plan of action is not yet fully worked out, and there remains some doubt as to how we are going to proceed. We hesitate until we can see our way more clearly. (Unfortunately, reluctance to start anything is a weakness many of us have.)

It is this inability to make a decision as to what we want or what to do that keeps us from achieving. To make any changes, to accomplish anything, we must put aside all further reflection and come to a decision. Nothing happens until we do.

Ideas need life breathed into them through definite plans for immediate action.

The more we deliberate about the best way of getting started, the less likely we are to get started at all. We will not get anything accomplished unless we start it, and we cannot start it until we make up our mind to start, and we cannot make up our mind until we end our reluctance to start. It's a "Catch-22" situation. Any decision we make will not be firm until we do something about it, and the longer we put off doing something, the more shaky our decision becomes.

We change and grow through action. It is vitally important to *make* a decision, but until we *act* on the decision it remains a matter of "I would like to."

Beginning a project or activity is only half the formula for achievement. Getting things finished, once we have them started, is largely a matter of persistence. Persistence, like any other characteristic, is an acquired habit.

To develop initiative and persistence:
1. Make a decision without hesitation.
2. Having once made the decision, don't waste time reviewing it.
3. Act promptly upon the decision.
4. Have no doubts about the decision.
5. Maintain incentive by keeping our goal constantly before us.
6. Make positive affirmations regarding the project or activity. Use the words "I enjoy" frequently, rather than "I hate" or "I dislike."

To manage ourselves, we must learn to concentrate, for without the power of concentration, self-management is impossible. If we lack the power of concentration, we will fall prey to every whim; if we possess it, we are in control. Concentration is the focusing of all our attention on one objective and refusing to consider anything that is not pertinent to the objective.

There are many examples of our *lack* of concentration, of allowing our environment to distract us. For instance, we have decided to answer a long over-due letter. We haven't decided what we are going to say. As we sit at our desk, our eyes wander to the wall. A picture is crooked. We get up and straighten it. We sit down again. Maybe we could think better with a clean desk. So we proceed to put things away, sharpen a few pencils, water a plant that's on our desk, empty the wastepaper basket. While we're in the kitchen emptying the wastepaper basket, we put a few dishes in the dishwasher and make ourselves a cup of tea. While we're waiting for the water to boil, we water the plants in the kitchen. (We must make a note of getting more plant food and perhaps more plants). One thought leads to another. In the meantime, we have strayed far from our original objective — writing a letter.

An intense interest in the subject or activity is essential for concentration. When we absorb ourself in a particular subject or project, we are oblivious to everything around us.

Concentration and singleness of purpose are closely associated. Lacking interest, concentration is almost impossible. It is difficult to focus all our attention on a subject that is vague. The more definite we can make our objective, the easier it will be to concentrate. If our objective is fuzzy, if there is an elusive quality about it, then concentration is difficult. We must have something we can hold on to. Our objective must be clear cut. This can be done by breaking it down and concentrating on a small part at a time.

For the past two years I have been writing two-minute transcripts for a radio feature. One day I decided to write a book. I thought it would simply be a matter of compiling my transcripts, but I soon realized that I was wrong. For the next six months I did everything *but* write my book. I continued to give seminars, talks, opened a center for self-improvement, wrote my radio scripts, but I could never manage to find the time to sit down each day and write. I gathered data for the book — two boxes full. I made notes — in the car, restaurants, during the night, and early morning.

I realized one day that I lacked singleness of purpose. The idea of writing a book was too overwhelming for me to cope with. I had not really convinced myself that I was writing a book. I couldn't seem to concentrate.

I am intensely interested in the subject of self-improvement, but writing a book on the subject was something else. I would sit down at my typewriter with good intentions, but I ended up filling the wastepaper basket faster than I filled a page. I found my thoughts wandering. Everything became a distraction. Mentally, the book was lacking definite form.

Then, one day, a brief conversation with a friend surfaced. He said, "When you write a book, you don't start with Chapter 1. Just start writing." Once I stopped thinking about the *completed* book, I had no problem concentrating.

I also started making the affirmation, "I enjoy writing my book." When I finally convinced my subconscious mind that I *was* writing a book, I no longer had to force myself to write. It became the most important thing in my life.

When we doubt our ability to succeed in any project on which we are concentrating, we will find it difficult to focus our attention. I doubted my ability to write a book many times, and this set up fear and worry in my mind. When I entertained these doubts, I lost the power of concentration.

Like most characteristics, the extent of our power to concentrate is an acquired habit. To strengthen our ability to concentrate, we have to maintain a deep interest in our objective. This will stimulate us to act regardless of the fact that we have feelings of inadequacy and frustration. That is why it is important to plan for each day, and concentrate *only* on top priorities. When we extend ourselves into other activities, we weaken our power to achieve our objective. Concentrate on one goal at a time, instead of scattering our efforts, and we will be successful, for a goal brings singleness of purpose.

Success
Is
Predictable!

When we decide on what it is we desire most at this time.

When we write down each day the five or more important tasks or projects we want to accomplish.

When we do something each day that pertains to our goal.

When we spend sometime each day on our positive affirmations.

When we eliminate thoughts of doubt in regard to achieving our goal.

When we forget our past mistakes and failures.

When we can persist in spite of obstacles.

117

Part Two

"We never get a second chance to make a first impression."

Back to Basics

CHAPTER SEVEN

THE first impression of the kind of person we are is made by the way we look, for clothes reflect what we think we are and what we want to be. If we are well put together, we start with an advantage.

We all have experienced times when we didn't feel good about our appearance, and consequently, our thoughts focused all day on how we looked, and made us uncomfortable in the presence of others.

When we are satisfied with the way we look, we have an inner security which allows us to concentrate on things other than ourselves.

Our self-confidence, or lack of, is very evident in the selection of our wardrobe. To be well dressed doesn't require a closet bursting with clothes, but rather having a few-well-chosen pieces in which we always feel at ease.

Suitable clothing brings out our best personality traits and physical features. They make us feel our very best. Well-designed garments do not go out of style as quickly, and we don't tire of them as readily as clothes designed for the moment.

A friend once said to me, "One of the objections I have about going back to work is that every day I would have to decide what to wear. Just the thought of it tires me out."

Through wise planning we can choose a few garments that go together and look like many. We can anticipate our needs and avoid last-minute shopping which is always expensive.

Since no one can afford to throw out everything they own, we have to look for ways to adapt the clothes already in our wardrobe.

There are two ways to plan a wardrobe; one, we can take inventory of our present wardrobe and then determine what additional clothes we need for our activities; second, we can consider our activities and the clothes we need for them, then determine what clothes we already have that are suitable for our needs. Then we can plan what new items we must have.

The type and amount of clothes we need for our lifestyle is the first consideration. We will be more realistic with ourselves and won't confuse needs and desires, nor will we tend to justify keeping some of the garments in our present wardrobe that may be of no use to us.

After deciding the type and amount of clothes that are important for our activities, we can then inventory what we have in our existing wardrobe. We need to determine how each article can fit into our lifestyle. We may also realize that some things we own are not worth the space they take up in our closet or drawers and could be better used by someone else. After determining what is needed and what we have, then the major planning job begins, that of figuring out additional items needed and how to acquire them.

It takes time to make an inventory of our wardrobe, so this task should be accomplished on a day that we haven't too many things planned. Begin by emptying all items from drawers and closet, making note of anything that is at the cleaners or in the laundry which should be considered. Items that are good, but suitable for another season, should be stored elsewhere. We don't want to confuse the issue. It is less confusing if we deal with only one season at a time.

Try on everything, and do it in front of a full length mirror, wearing the shoes we usually wear with that particular outfit. While we have an outfit on, experiment with different accessories, trying every blouse, shirt and sweater with every skirt we have, listing the accessories we need to update each outfit.

As we try on each outfit, we need to ask ourselves these questions:

1. Is it in style?
2. Is it becoming to me?
3. Does it fit well?
4. Will it be suitable for at least one of my activities?
5. Is it in good condition?

If we can answer 'yes' to all counts, it can be put back in the closet.

At this point, we are ready to consider what additional clothes we need for the coming season. Making a list of our activities and also our clothing inventory will simplify things.

The most expensive items in our wardrobe are those that are never worn, no matter how inexpensive they are. A guideline to follow when planning our wardrobe:

1. Avoid impulse buying.
2. Buy clothes that fit our lifestyle.
3. Look for clothes that can do double duty.
4. Knowing what we want and don't have in accessories.
5. Be on the lookout for interesting belts or scarves that will update our outfits.

If our present wardrobe is a rainbow of color and we find ourselves changing purses often to match our clothes or keeping our coat buttoned so it won't clash with what we're wearing underneath, or we find ourselves buying a different item and then having to buy other things to go with it, now is a good time to get ourselves out of this muddle. Deciding on a master color plan is vital. It may take a few seasons to get it all together. It is necessary to plan our purchases carefully so that one-color accessories at least for the fall and winter season will be right for all our clothes.

It is wise to select a basic color, such as black, navy blue, or brown, and build around it. If our outfits are all bright colors, we should consider dark or neutral colors for accessories, but if we prefer plain colors for our clothes, we can use bright bold accessories.

Color can make the eye see things differently. For example, if two women wore the identical dress in the same style, and one was bright red and the other black, we would find that the woman wearing the red dress appears to be larger. Light and bright colors seem to advance and make things appear larger. Dark shades and muted colors, on the other hand, seem to recede and produce the effect of reducing size and creating more clearly defined outlines.

At one time the basic *black* dress was a necessity, but there are many other basic colors

127

to choose from. Black is the most slenderizing color we can wear. However, black tends to drain color from the face and accentuates facial lines. The one effective way black can be worn is to put white or a color near the face.

White reflects light. It is clean and fresh looking and it is kind to the face. It is the opposite of black in that it rounds out the figure. It's hard to understand why dress manufacturers put white belts on a size 18 dress, but they do, and large women continue to wear them.

Brown is probably the most underrated color in the spectrum. It is an elegant and distinctive color.

Beige combines the color and versatility of black and white. Beige also compliments most women. However, it is not the best color for the woman who is overweight.

Grey, close to the face, is like black. It is an unforgiving color. To be worn effectively, it should be worn with white near the face.

Navy blue is more flattering to the face than black or grey and is more slimming than white or beige.

Clothes in a basic color are worn longer than bright or pastels. Neutral colors are also easier to accessorize.

Because most figures are less than perfect, it is important to choose lines and shapes that are flattering to us. If a woman is very tall or very short, too thin or too heavy, there are some guidelines to follow:

Tall women can combine colors, mix prints and solids, add bracelets, belts and scarves to break up the long head-to-toe line. Shoes with lower heels are her best bet, but she should avoid flat-heeled shoes which are less flattering to the leg. Skirts can be pleated, full, flared or A-line. Avoid the fitted lines, as they tend to accentuate height. A two-piece, belted shirtwaist is a good silhouette.

Short women can wear one-piece dresses of one color, with narrow belts of the same fabric. Keep accessories small. Avoid a waist and skirt in contrasting colors, full sleeves, shiny fabric, large prints or wide stripes.

If a woman is heavy, she should start with the right foundation. A lightly shaping all-in-one garment will give her a long, smooth line. She should choose one that is zipperless, if possible, looking for fashion fabrics that have some body and won't cling, fabric that can hold a silhouette but will not conform completely with her figure's outline. Stay away from contrasting colors in bodice and skirt, and avoid belts, unless they are narrow or the same color as the dress they will be worn with. If her legs are heavy, she should wear sheer support hose. Stay away from black hosiery, as it attracts attention to heavy legs.

For the very *thin* woman, bulky fabrics like tweeds, patterned fabrics, fabrics with texture or sheen, such as velvets, corduroy and mohair mixtures are best. Soft draping fabrics, such as qiana or tissue flannel, are good if they are used for full gathered styles. Her kind of dress is the shirt-waist with its full, long sleeves, gathered skirt. She can add inches (or so it seems) by wearing wide belts. A scarf at the neckline is one of the best ways to soften a thin neck.

For a well-rounded wardrobe, we should have at least four skirts, one grey, a navy blue, a black, brown or beige, and one tweed. A skirt is a foundation. It's the base from which we work. Being on the bottom, skirts should be heavier, either in texture or color, than the top.

Narrow skirts are best worn by a woman with a slim figure, as are skirts pleated all around. If she has full hips, she will look better in skirts with a slight flare such as an A-line or one with low pleats and a stitched top. Tall slender women can wear almost any type of skirt, although straight skirts will emphasize height.

Points to be checked in the fit of a skirt: there should be enough fullness to prevent strain, wrinkles or pulling up when we sit down. The waist band should fit snugly to our figure.

Blouses and shirts can change the appearance of a suit, skirt, or pants to make them suitable for several occasions. Coordinating the blouse to the skirt or other clothing with which they are to be worn, either by color or texture or design. A well-chosen blouse should be right with several items in our wardrobe.

We should check to see that:

- The collar fits smoothly and does not wrinkle or stand away from the body.
- The fullness at the bust is adequate with no pull wrinkles below the bust.
- The blouse is smooth across the back of the shoulders.
- There is no strain across any center opening.
- The length is suitable for us. If it is an overblouse, it should not be so short that it rides up above the waistline with movement, nor so long that it looks awkward.

In considering dresses for the basic wardrobe, we don't need more than three or four. Avoid buying dresses that leave no room for change, for a dress we can't change becomes boring. If the dress comes with a belt, cut off the little string loops. Manufacturers put them on dresses to keep belts from getting lost while they are hanging in the stores.

131

A good basic wardrobe should consist of clothing with the look of simplicity, clean lines, good tailoring and good fabric.

If we feel the price is right for the quality of the fabric and workmanship, and other features meet our approval, try it on and study it in a full length mirror.

1. Ask in what way does this dress improve my appearance?
2. Are there any features about it that make me feel less attractive?
3. Is it comfortable as I walk, sit, and bend my arms?
4. Are alterations necessary? How much will it cost?

If we cannot find a dress that fits completely, it is usually best to choose one that fits the upper part of the body as the skirt is easier to fit than the waist.

Because a coat is usually the most expensive garment we purchase, we must choose our coat carefully, and consider color before making any garment selection. It should be an investment item, as fine fabric and tailoring cannot be purchased cheaply.

A good fit in a coat or suit is essential for comfort, appearance and good service. The points to check in the fit of a coat and suit are:

- The collar should fit close to the neck at the back and the side.
- Shoulders and hips should have a smooth fit.

- Sleeves should be large enough for clothing worn underneath.

A suit is the mainstay of our wardrobe. It is the garment we will probably wear two or three times a week. A suit, chosen in a medium weight fabric in any of the basic colors, is the way to go. Accessorized with scarves, blouses, sweaters, or jewelry, a suit can be worn from morning till night.

It's important for us to remember that quality, not quantity, is the rule to follow in selecting our clothes. We will save money and be more distinctive with a few well-made clothes than a closet full of inexpensive purchases.

Our accessories will be the ingredient that make our outfits look great, greater or the greatest. Paying close attention to fashion magazines and store window displays will give us new ideas in accessorizing. Skirts and blouses coordinated with belts, scarves, and jewelry will give our wardrobe versatility. There are three things to consider when buying accessories:

1. What will I wear it with?
2. Does it go with anything else?
3. Does it go with me?

In the final analysis, a good basic wardrobe should consist of clothing with the look of simplicity, clean lines, good tailoring and good fabric, and clothes that will give us the feeling of confidence because we know we look good.

One thing is for certain, we never get a second chance to make a first impression.

136

*"From birth to
age eighteen,
a girl needs good parents.
From eighteen
to thirty-five,
she needs good looks.
From thirty-five
to fifty-five,
she needs a good
personality.
From fifty-five on,
she needs good cash."*

SOPHIE TUCKER

What's in a Name?

CHAPTER EIGHT

ALONG with having good cash, a woman, today, needs good creditworthiness.

Statistics show that women are awesome consumers, making 65 to 70 percent of the buying decisions. But when there is a divorce, the husband walks away with the credit cards along with the credit history. The wife is left sitting like a teenager because everything has always been in her husband's name.

A typical story is that of a woman, who at forty-five years of age, never held a job, taken out a loan, or had credit in her name.

Now divorced, she has no credit history. Even though she had recently started a job, a bank turned down her application for a credit card.

This might not have happened had some of the recently enacted federal laws on credit been around while she was married. Under the Equal Credit Opportunity Act, she could have been taking steps to assure that she shared her husband's record of promptly paid debts.

The increasing divorce rate, and the fact that the average woman out-lives her husband, puts many women in a similar position.

Many of us tend to think of money in nickel and dime terms. The grand plans of investment, mortgages, and even savings often escapes us. We don't have much experience with expense accounts, tax shelters and pension plans. We don't do too much planning for the future — we feel that someone will come along and take care of it.

According to one bank official, "The problem with women and credit today, is not with the credit industry, as it was in the past, but with the women themselves. Many married women don't understand why it's necessary to have credit in their names. Their lives are going smoothly as is, and they see no reason to be concerned. There's not enough knowledge on the part of women on what that second credit history can do."

Under the new law, new charge accounts and loans will be reported in the wife's own name as well as the husband's. But the wife's present accounts will remain in her husband's name unless she takes positive action to change it. The credit history continues to be reported under the husband's name. It simply adds the wife's name to the account, as someone equally entitled to the credit history.

Today a woman doesn't have to state if she is married, or her husband's name, if she is. She gives her name as "Mary Smith Brown," not Mrs. John Brown." Otherwise, the credit information continues to be filed under the husband's name. Under this law, women do not have to work outside the home in order to get the benefit of a credit history, although a woman who is married and unemployed still won't get a separate credit card from her husband.

Any woman who has tried to get credit in the past, knows how difficult it was, partly due to our traditional role of dependence on men and partly because of a failure of some credit officers to realize that the tradition is changing.

In 1975, Congress passed the Equal Credit Opportunity Act which mandated that:

- You can't be refused credit just because you're a woman.
- You can't be refused credit just because you're single, married, separated, divorced, or widowed.

141

- You can't be refused credit because a creditor decides you're of child-bearing age and, as a consequence, won't count your income.
- You can't be refused credit because a creditor won't count income you receive regularly from alimony or child support.
- You can have credit in your name if you're creditworthy.
- When you apply for your own credit and rely on your own income, information about your spouse or his co-signature can be required only under certain circumstances.
- You can keep your own accounts and your own credit history if your marital status changes.
- You can build up your own credit record because new accounts must be carried in names of husband and wife if both use the account or are liable on it.

The Equal Credit Opportunity Act does not lessen the importance of money management and good financial credentials in establishing and using credit. The law provides that equal consideration be given to all creditworthy applicants.

According to one source, creditors choose various ways to rate our creditworthiness. They may ask about our finances: how much we earn, what kind of savings and investments we have, what our other sources of income are. They may look for signs of reliability: our occupation, how long we've been employed, how long we've lived at the same address, whether we own our own home or rent. Credit officers look for someone who has worked in the same job at least six months. They may also examine our credit record: how much we owe, how often we borrowed, and how we've managed past debts. A good credit history can supersede the need to have been established in one job. That's where a second credit history can mean so much to a married woman. If we have a good credit history, the credit officer is less concerned with how much money we make. A good credit history usually includes credit from at least three sources.

With no credit history, the best place to start is with a department store credit card. The department store is sure to report your performance to the local credit bureau.

A woman starting with no credit history needs everything going for her, so we must be sure to put down every strength we can think of on the application, even if the information isn't requested. Longtime residence in the community, former employment and other financial

A good credit history can
supersede the need to have
been established in one job.

resources beyond job income can make the difference. The creditor wants to be assured of two things: our ability to repay our debts and our willingness to do so.

Recently a story appeared in the newspaper telling of the plight of a woman who had no credit card. She said, "My husband and I pay cash for everything we buy and pride ourselves on the fact that we owe no one."

Because of a family emergency, she had to make an unexpected trip to another part of the country. She said, "I had no difficulty paying for my air-line ticket by check, but when I got to my destination, I found I couldn't rent a car. No credit card, no car, period. I offered to pay in advance, and leave a deposit, all to no avail." She felt she had been discriminated against because she was a woman.

She was informed that she was discriminated against, but not because she was a woman. It was because she was a member of a minority group - the minority with no credit cards. To car-rental companies, which deal exclusively with the credit card set, she and all like her are simply non-persons.

Car-rental companies will not rent a car to someone without an acceptable credit card until they make a check of their creditworthiness. This may require a verification of employment, residence, telephone listing, and perhaps even bank references. This can take from one to three days and can only be done during normal business hours, not in the evening or during the weekend. So if we want to rent a car locally without a credit card, we must make arrangements in advance. If we are out of town, we may as well forget it.

Today, department stores in larger cities will not accept a personal check unless you have two forms of identifications. You cannot check into some hotels and pay for your lodging by check unless you have a credit card for identification.

Several years ago, I made a trip to Chicago. I had room accommodations in one of the large hotels downtown. When I arrived, the desk clerk asked me how I would be paying for the room. I said, "by check." He said, "Do you have a major credit card?" I said, "No." That was the end of that. I could not get a room without two forms of identifications. It was eleven o'clock at night, and I said, "What will I do?" His answer was, "I haven't the slightest idea." When I regained my composure, I asked him for one dollar in dimes. I went to the telephone booth and proceeded to call other hotels. Fortunately, for me, I found a hotel that would accept me without a credit card. That night, in the quiet of my hotel room, I made a silent vow that I would make every effort to obtain a credit card as soon as possible.

Any woman, single or married, with or without a job, who is not building her own credit history, should make that one of her first goals.

One result of the new laws and the changing times has been that more women are applying for their own credit card accounts. As one bank official remarked, "Having a credit card does give a woman clout." It also creates a feeling of security - especially in front of a disinterested hotel clerk.

Part Three

Latch on to
the Positive!

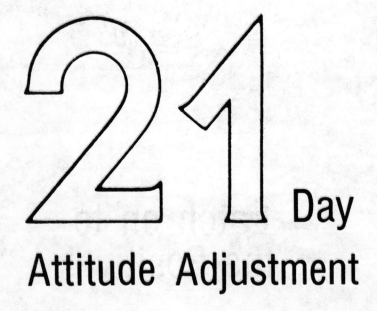

21Day

Attitude Adjustment

During the course of a day we are constantly bombarded by thoughts of all kinds. These thoughts determine, to a great degree, the condition of our relationships with others, and the degree of our achievements.

It takes about 21 days to break a habit, and about 21 days to form a new one.

On the following pages are concepts and ideas to help make positive adjustments in our thinking regarding ourselves and our capabilities.

We have been given our own identity, our own uniqueness. Never before has anyone appeared on the face of the earth, with a combination of our qualities, abilities, talents and attitudes. No single snowflake is ever duplicated, much less a human being.

Success attracts success, and all the laws of life will work for us if we think positively. We were made to succeed, and as in the physical law that no two objects can occupy the same space at the same time, so is it a law in the mental realm that destructive thoughts of failure cannot find room simultaneously with the constructive thoughts for success.

153

Self-Awareness

MILLIONS of women go all the way through life blaming their mediocrity on their lack of talent.

According to the experts, it is not the lack of talent but the failure to recognize and develop talent that is our basic problem.

William James concluded that, *"Most people live, whether physically, intellectually or morally, in a very restricted circle of their potential being. They make use of a very small portion of their possible consciousness, and of their soul's resources in general, much like a man who, out of his whole bodily organism, should get into a habit of using and moving only his little finger. Great emergencies and crises show us how greater our vital resources are than we had supposed."*

Experts on creativity are convinced that most of us have enormous untapped creative abilities.

We all have the potential to be whatever we desire to be. But it's those who are unable to motivate themselves that must be satisfied with mediocrity, no matter how imposing their other talents are.

Setting up challenges for ourselves by establishing goals will bring some of our potential to the surface.

Eliminate the Negative

EACH of us constantly uses the law of action and reaction, whether we are aware of it or not. If we wish to enjoy more success in life, we must consciously and deliberately take charge of our thoughts and feelings and direct them toward success.

If we want success of any kind, we must begin today to eliminate negative words, or they will tend to destroy our enthusiasm and our progress.

Without a high regard for ourselves and, consequently, for what we can do, we will find we lack the security and confidence in ourselves necessary to achieve. Negative words are so natural for us that, most of the time, we are unaware that we use them.

How often do we say, "Everything happens to me," "I just don't seem to get anywhere," "I'm at a loss as to what to do?"

James Allen said, *"All that we achieve in life, and all that we fail to achieve, is the direct result of our thoughts."*

We must choose to believe that something good can happen and is happening, rather than taking the negative approach that something is bound to happen, but it won't be good. Our greatest power is our capacity to choose.

No Freebies

MOST of us put limitations upon ourselves by our habitual pattern of thinking that includes small everyday happenings. We don't allow ourselves into the boundless realm of creative thought, where we can envision wonderful experiences, better jobs, and bigger incomes. Our pattern of thought binds us to lives of inactivity and limitations.

We are proficient at thinking small, but it takes a truly expanded mind to think big thoughts.

Many of the beliefs we have were put there by the people who existed in our world when we were children. Some of us were told it was wrong to want to be rich, and that money wasn't important.

We must break this pattern of thinking. If we don't think money is important, or if we say, "Money is not important," we can be sure that we won't have any.

There is nothing wrong with wanting to better ourselves. It is not wrong to want a great deal of money. Think of all the wonderful things we can do with it. Think of the things we could do for others.

We must begin to change our mental concepts.

We have the right to demand the best that life has to offer.

Seed Thoughts

OUR mind can be compared to a garden. We can cultivate it intelligently or allow it to grow wild. But whether we plant or not, something will grow.

Many of us spend a good deal of time thinking about the negative aspects of our lives, the lack, limitations, and disappointments. The thoughts that take root in our mind will bear fruit after their kind.

We create our own future thought by thought. By planting the seeds of success, we begin to do the things that will attract success.

Everyday it is essential to plant the seeds of health, happiness, success and friendship. In doing this we eliminate from our mind all concern about our conditions or circumstances. No matter who we are, or where we are, we continue to plant the positive seeds in our mind, and if we leave them undisturbed by doubt, they will germinate and grow.

When we say, "There's no way out," we will get no response from our subconscious mind.

If we want this powerful creative mind to work for us, we must plant the positive seeds.

These thoughts become real. Our desires are seed thoughts that sprout and grow and bear fruit.

Letting Go

MANY of us carry the memory of past mistakes with us and waste time and energy reviewing them. Our biggest mistake is to continually recall our mistakes, our failures, and constantly checking out our yesterdays.

To be successful in our endeavors and happy, our expectations for the future must be positive. When we think over and over about the mistakes of the past, they become more and more a part of us.

There are lessons that can be learned from our mistakes, but after we have learned from them, we should let them go.

Everything that we have ever experienced is within our mind. We can never erase it, but we can keep from giving it life by not giving it the energy from our thoughts.

Whenever we dwell on our past mistakes and failures, they are resurrected and become our future. The same holds true for our successes.

We must forget the failures of yesterday and the fears of tomorrow — they don't exist. We should think of today and achieve something today.

Self-Belief

To be a confident person, we must dominate our doubts, but a great majority of us let our doubts rule us.

We cannot think success and failure at the same time. Either one or the other must dominate. Positive thinking brings on the confidence we desire. Negative thinking brings on the feelings of doubt and fear.

We all have inadequacies, we can't excel in everything. When we accept the fact that we do, then it must hold true for others.

When we have faith in ourselves, our abilities, our talents, we go on handling our affairs in a satisfying way, but as soon as we start doubting ourselves, our abilities, our talents, we will experience problems.

Doubts are destructive because they destroy our motivation.

Our mind can focus on only one thing at a time. If we fill our mind with confident thoughts, we will leave no room for self-doubt.

Our life is an individual responsibility, an individual opportunity, and an individual experience. Whatever we choose to think will become a reality in time.

Days of Our Lives

THE riches that each of us starts with is our lifetime. All the seconds, minutes, hours, days, months and years we are alive.

But how many of us are excited about life or appreciate each day?

There is an old legend about Aaron, a fisherman who lived on the banks of a river. Walking home, with his eyes half closed one evening after a hard day's toil, he was dreaming of what he would do when he became rich. Suddenly, his foot struck against a leather pouch filled with, what seemed to him small stones. Absentmindedly he picked up the pouch and began throwing the pebbles into the water.

"When I am rich," he said to himself, "I'll have a large house." And he threw a stone. He threw another and thought, "I'll have servants and wine and rich food." This went on until only one stone was left. As Aaron held it in his hand, a ray of light caught it and made it sparkle. He realized then that it was a valuable gem, that he had been throwing away the real riches in his hand while he dreamed idly of unreal riches in the future.

Learning to take hold of our present moment is the first step to living happily, instead of postponing our pleasure until we are too old to enjoy it.

Time is our most precious and priceless element to use, not to let slip away and lose

Habit Pattern

As creatures of habit, most of us follow the path of least resistance. It is so much easier to awaken each day at a given time and look forward to a day of routine and schedules than to awaken earlier and do something different.

Some of us are haunted by a suppressed dissatisfaction with our daily life. We have a feeling that we are leaving something undone, something we always meant to do when we had more time, yet we make little effort to find out what it is. A look at our calendar tells us that we don't have the time for new ventures or old dreams. We allow the calendar to fool us into thinking we have no more energy. We can finally give in and take it easy.

On the positive side, however, it may occur to us that we have another fifteen or twenty years of life ahead of us. If this be the case, then what about these remaining years? Maybe it's time to dust off those old dreams.

Grandma Moses achieved greatness as an artist at a time when many women are being tucked into their rocking chairs.

In order to make the most of everyday we must look for opportunities — make the most of ourselves.

What ever point we are at, we should strive to get the most out of it.

Success Ingredients

BEGINNING a project is only half of the formula of achievement. Getting things finished, once we have started, is a matter of persistence.

Many of us reach a point where we seem to be defeated and we give up, when, with just a little more persistence, we could have succeeded.

An extraordinary personal history of multiple failures was experienced by a man who lost his job in 1832 - defeated for legislature in 1832 - he failed in business in 1833 - elected to legislature in 1834 - the woman he loved died in 1835 - he had a nervous breakdown in 1836 - defeated for speaker of the House in 1838 - defeated for nomination for Congress in 1843 - elected to Congress in 1846 - lost nomination in 1848 - rejected for land officer in 1849 - defeated for Senate in 1854 - defeated for nomination for vice-president in 1856 - again defeated for Senate in 1858. However, in 1860 Abraham Lincoln was elected President of the United States.

Each time we feel like giving up, we should take a fresh look at what prompted us to decide upon our goal. Thinking about it can give us back our enthusiasm.

We never know, for sure, the distance between failure and success. In many cases the two are separated by the length of one negative word - "discouragement."

10

Self-Acceptance

IT has been established that the limitations which restrict us from our full potential are caused by a limited self-image.

Many of us emphasize what we are not, rather than what we are. We dwell on our shortcomings and faults. We exaggerate the abilities of others and criticize our lack of them. We measure our weaknesses against their strengths. But, we see in others only the surface of assurance. We would judge ourselves less severely if we realized that. Everyone bears the scars of many failures.

At some time or other we reach a point where we must have a certain amount of respect and consideration for ourselves. If life is to be an enjoyable experience, the first person to get along with and to like is ourselves.

Self-acceptance isn't passive. We must affirm everyday that we like and accept ourselves, stop criticizing ourselves and look for our strengths.

Shakespeare said, *"We know what we are, but we know not what we can be."*

Real success is not possible until we gain a high degree of self-acceptance.

Good Relationships

Each of us experiences many relationships. These relationships may vary from a deep to the most superficial involvement.

If we want our relationships with others to contribute to our growth rather than hinder it, we should begin by taking stock of our present relationships.

We all know certain friends or acquaintances who affect us in a positive way, and then there are others who can depress us.

We should ask ourselves: Who brings out the best in me, qualities I do not usually use? Which person, or persons, stimulate me? Which person makes me feel that they really care about me? Which person makes me feel less vulnerable? Who makes me feel more vital, more alive, and more myself?

Anyone of us, who is making an effort toward growth, must be concerned with the people with whom we have relationships.

We should select our encounters so that they become opportunities for personal growth. Developing those relationships which hold within them the promise of helping us unfold our own uniqueness. For we are shaped, to a great extent, by our relationships.

Break the Habit

IT'S within the reach of each of us to make our lives more meaningful. Because we are creatures of habit, most of us keep doing the same things over and over again. We see the same friends each weekend, take the same old vacations. Consequently, we get stuck in a rut.

We find excuses why we shouldn't do something. Some of us become very proficient at finding excuses for not doing things. By the time we're sixty, we look back and all we find are excuses and no interesting experiences. We have to start thinking of reasons why we can do something — not why we can't.

Each day we should do something different. Something trivial, that will give us momentary pleasure, such as buying flowers for ourselves, going for a walk after lunch, taking a bath by candlelight. We should try to do one pleasurable thing every day for a month. And not repeating any of these. This in turn will lead us to search out larger pleasures.

We should think about the kind of person we want to be, about all the details of that kind of person — how we would dress, where we would work, the car we would drive, what our lifestyle would be. Having that picture in mind, we could move step by step toward our goal.

Enthusiasm

EACH of us is capable of enthusiasm, but, like confidence, we must create it. The only way we can do that is by changing our thoughts.

Enthusiasm is the quality that will keep us young and vital. It is also the important ingredient for success. As Emerson put it, *"Nothing great was ever achieved without enthusiasm."*

Enthusiasm can come from an idea we have about how we can accomplish something. It can come from our expectations.

We condition our mind in the first few moments after we awaken. It is important to choose only positive thoughts in those first few moments of awareness.

So, instead of lying in bed thinking about all the gloomy things that might happen or could happen, we need to think of all the good things we have, such as family, friends, a healthy body, a powerful mind.

One thing for us to remember is that our thoughts upon awakening tend to affect our entire day. We always have a choice. We can decide to think discouraging thoughts that depress us, or we can think positive thoughts that will fill us with enthusiasm for the day. Our continual choice will determine the quality of our days and also of our life.

Self-Motivation

ONE of the prime factors in achievement is motivation. No matter how intelligent or talented we are, how many opportunities come our way, if we are not motivated, we will accomplish very little.

Millions of people work all their lives with no stronger motivation than that of acquiring the necessities of life, such as a roof over their heads, food on the table and clothes on their backs.

Without a strong desire for more, nothing happens. It is the motivating force within us.

First, we must decide on the changes we want to make, and have a strong feeling about the changes. Desire these changes. If the changes include a different place to live, a new job, the desire for it will be our starting point. If our desire is strong enough we will be motivated to make decisions.

We must decide, at any age or stage of life, in choosing our course, that we will be doing what we want, not what someone else decides is best for us.

Our mind reacts to that which is desirable and attainable.

Free to be Me

IT'S easy to think that at times we don't have the opportunity to live our own lives. Family, employers, and friends, tell us how we should live.

I am reminded of a story I read as a child.

"A man and his son were traveling to a distant town. They only had one horse between them. So the old man rode upon the horse, and the young boy walked beside them.

"As they passed through the first town, the people stood around and shamed the old man for riding on the horse and making the little boy walk. The old man got off the horse and let the little boy ride. They came to another town, and the people chided the boy for riding on the horse while the old man had to walk. So the man got on the horse, along with the little boy, and they both rode on the horse. When they arrived at the third town, the townspeople said, 'Look at that old man and that young boy both riding on that poor old horse.' Thereupon, the man and the boy got off the horse, made a sling, and proceeded to carry the horse."

This story clearly illustrates that there is no such thing as a universal rule of conduct.

There are many people in this world, and we don't have to try to please everyone. What might be irritating to one person can be enjoyable to another.

16
Goal-Setting

ONE of the essential ingredients in achieving is a belief in ourselves.

Small goals, regularly achieved, give us the experience of success and develops our self-confidence. If we achieve success in a few things, it will give us the encouragement to achieve more.

To try to achieve too many goals at one time, to scatter our thoughts and efforts, is to risk disappointment.

As soon as we begin this kind of program, we will find ourselves more confident, because we are directing our thoughts along this channel.

To keep the belief alive in ourselves, we must:

- Not confide our secret innermost dreams to other people.
- Keep our mind on our goal, not on the obstacles we must overcome.
- Each night, upon retiring, we should spend a few moments visualizing the goal we want to achieve.

We will feel more and more confident if we can look to the future with hope that we will become the person we would like to be, and with the accepted belief that we will achieve our goal.

Think Success

WE all at one time or another have failed in some undertaking which gives us a feeling of uncertainty. Some of us are ashamed of the failures and let past failures control our lives.

We do this at a time when we are working to reach a goal. We re-live them and make them our present. We become fearful that we will fail again in our present undertaking.

But, in remembering our past mistakes, we are, in truth, reliving them.

The greatest failure of all is to be afraid to make a mistake. If we rise above fear, we automatically gain confidence.

We should visualize the things we would like to see in our life. Forgetting about the things that happened in the past. In place of them we should create mentally the conditions we would like to see.

The key to being what we can be is simply making a decision as to what we want of life. Plan it out in detail. Picture it. See ourselves as we are now, doing those things we have always wanted to do. We must make them real in our mind's eye. Feel them — believe them — especially at the moment of going to sleep. A mental image provides the basis for everything we want.

18
Power of Thought

SOME of us feel that we are held back from living our life as we want to because, "It's too late," or we spend so much time complaining that, "I've wasted so many years," that we have no desire or energy to make a change.

To achieve anything worthwhile in life, it is imperative that we take a positive attitude toward ourselves and what we would like to achieve. It is impossible for us to achieve any success with a low self-image.

Through belief in ourselves, in our ability, we will be able to succeed in our individual work.

The power of thought, and the accurate response of our creative mind, are reflected in these lines:

If you think you are beaten, you are.
If you think you dare not, you don't.
If you like to win, but you think you can't,
It's almost certain you won't.
If you think you'll lose, you're lost,
For out of the world we find,
Success begins with a person's will.
It's all in the state of mind.

Thought is the source of all wealth, all success, all achievement. Our dominant thoughts determine our individuality, our career, our daily life.

19
Inner Thoughts

WHO we are, what we have, are the result of our thoughts. Our life, through our thoughts, is in our hands. We can make it whatever we desire. We are free to make or mar, to build or destroy, to be strong or weak, happy or miserable, successful or unsuccessful. It's all a matter of channeling our thoughts.

We may say to ourselves, "I will fail, I can never succeed." If we continue to think along these lines, this defeatist attitude in due time will weaken us, paralyze our efforts, and bring failure into our life.

So, instead of the negative thought, "I will fail," replace it with the positive, "I will succeed." Everytime we do this, we push failure further and further away and establish the idea of success more firmly in our mind.

At a particular moment, the very next thought that crosses our mind can make us a different person, for we are the products of our thoughts.

It doesn't matter when or where the thought comes, whether it filters into our consciousness in the silence of our bedroom, or whether it comes to us in the noise of a busy day. If we hold onto the thought, it becomes a part of us and will, in time, become a reality in our life.

Within us lies the cause of whatever enters into our life.

Self-Confidence

THE first step towards eliminating a feeling of inferiority and replacing it with a feeling of confidence, is to be sure we have no time to waste in thinking about our inabilities.

Confidence is built upon successful experiences. Each little accomplishment we make towards our desired objective will add to our feeling of achievement, and to our confidence in our ability.

The next step is to make an effort to improve. We will never find life enjoyable if we have become satisfied with ourselves and our accomplishments. If we are not growing, we begin to lose our confidence. This happens to us after we stay home for many years. Like everything else in life, in order to keep it, we must work at it.

A powerful way to develop self-confidence is to feed our mind confident filled thoughts as we fall asleep at night. Psychologists believe that our last waking thoughts are the ones our subconscious mind accepts and acts upon.

And finally, we can never hope to acquire self-confidence if we don't appreciate ourselves and hold ourselves in high regard.

Self-confidence comes from knowing who we are and what we can achieve.

Self-Realization

BETWEEN our desire to succeed and our fear of failure, we can lead a miserable life.

The first requirement for success in the business world, as in our social life, is self-confidence. The second requirement is initiation. Many of us have ideas, but all too few of us have the confidence in ourselves to start anything.

The third requirement is the faith to do things in the face of obstacles.

We achieve self-confidence when we truly begin to discover ourselves, and realize that our capacities are greater than ever imagined.

Our mind contains within itself the power to create or destroy. Though invisible, its forces are awesome. Within our mind, lies the solution to our problems.

The mind is not only the power through which success and happiness are achieved, but it is also the source through which failure and frustration are experienced.

Confidence, courage, and faith come from knowing who we are and what is possible, and from belief in our own creativity.

Look
to
this
day . . .

For it is life, the very life of life.

In its brief course lie all the varieties

and realities of your existence:

The bliss of growth;

The glory of action;

The splendor of beauty;

For yesterday is already a dream,

and to-morrow is only a vision;

But to-day, well lived, makes every

yesterday a dream of happiness,

and every to-morrow a vision of hope.

Look well, therefore, to this day!

Such is the salutation of the dawn!

FROM THE SANSKRIT

BIBLIOGRAPHY

Allen, James: *As a Man Thinketh* (Alhambrah, California: Miller Books, 1976).

Kipling, Rudyard: *The Explorer* (New York: Double Day Doran & Co., 1929).

Maltz, Maxwell, M.D. F.I.C.S.: *Psycho-Cybernetics* (New York: Pocket Book *a division of Simon & Shuster, Inc., 1974).

William, John K.: *The Knack of Using Your Subconscious Mind* (New York: Prentice-Hall, Inc., 1952).

OTHER SUGGESTED READING

Baker, Samm Sinclair: *Conscious Happiness* (New York: Grosset & Dunlap, 1975).

Campbell, David: *If You Don't Know Where You're Going, You'll Probably End Up Somewhere Else* (Niles, Illinois: Argus Communications, 1974).

Gibran, Kahlil: *The Prophet* (New York: Random House, Inc. 1962).

Lakein, Alan: *How To Get Control of Your Life* (New York: Peter H. Wyden, Inc., 1974).

Maltz, Maxwell, M.D., F.I.C.S.: *Psycho-Cybernetics* (New York: Pocket Book *A division of Simon & Schuster, Inc., 27th printing, 1974).

Murphy, Joseph, D.R.S., Ph.D.: *The Power of Your Subconscious Mind* (New York: Prentice-Hall, Inc. 10th printing, 1971).

Overstreet, Bonaro W.: *Understanding Fear* (New York: Harper & Row, 1971).

Williams, John K.: *The Knack of Using Your Subconscious Mind* (New York: Prentice-Hall, Inc., 1952).

Photocomposition and printing by
The Herald Press
Pawtucket, Rhode Island

Joan Kennedy

is a lecturer, radio personality, and a member of
the National Speakers Association. She is a self-
made woman who exemplifies that attitude
and stick-to-it-iveness can bring about success.
Joan Kennedy has conducted seminars and
keynote addresses, around the country, for
conventions, sales meetings in addition to women's
clubs and organizations. Joan's philosophy has
helped many to become more effective on
their jobs and in living their lives. Her up-beat
message is applicable to women of all ages.
She shares her experiences, and explains how a
woman can raise her self-image along
with her potential.

Joan Kennedy's book is not only a 'how-to-do-it',
it's also a 'why-to-do-it' book.